TRAVELING

WHILE

BLACK AND LESBIAN

KHANYISA MNYAKA

Paperback: 978-0620823296
Ebook: B0945WR9HF

First paperback edition December 2018.

Edited by Khanyisa Mnyaka
Cover art by Karina Donis
Layout by Khanyisa Mnyaka

Contents

Introduction

Lesbian, black, woman and African – it's a lot, isn't it? A classmate during my MA Program at the University for Peace once observed:

"Khanyisa, you are black, woman and queer! That is all minority and oppression in one person".

She observed as if I did not know how the packaging of my being was representative of every oppressed community in the world. I just looked at her and said "yep". I know that she was not being malicious, but she had truly just comprehended the identities that I hold and how those are viewed in this world. My identities are the very first things that stick out when I present myself to the world. The blackness is always there, glistening in all its glory making sure that it can never be avoided.

Then there is the woman. I have never wanted to pretend to be a man, but I do love me a good browse at the H&M men's section and my wardrobe looks like it belongs to a Zara male manikin. Although I love to clothe myself in what is considered "men's clothes", there is no hiding the woman(ess) of this body. It is in my hips, the way they curve even when I tried to wear baggy clothes to hide them, it is in the hourglass shape that was handed down to me by the women in my ancestry line, these lips – full, soft, and juicy, just how the Gods intended. My breast, round, pear shaped perfections.

And then, there is the gayness, the lesbianism, the homosexuality of it all. It has taken a long time and a lot of work to be so comfortable with this identity and I am not about to start hiding it to make people comfortable. It's not that I walk into a room announcing, "This is Khanyisa, a homosexual, known as Lord of the lesbians to some" (although, I should try this one time and see how it goes). No, I enter the room as myself, completely comfortable in my own skin and when a moment to self-identify arrives (because it always does) then everyone will know that I am all glitter and rainbows.

1

I have not always walked the world with this level of confidence and self-awareness. I grew up in a country where there were and still are pockets of society that are disdained by each of my identities. In South Africa, not much is expected of you when you are a combination of these – hell, you don't expect much from yourself. You are happy that each day comes and goes and there is still air in your lungs. You work hard to be you, hard to be accepted and even harder to be loved. When the work you put in does not yield any fruit, you find yourself in a deep dark hole of depression. You not only have failed but *you* are failure imbodied. Your only option is to deny part of yourself, the parts that are just too unacceptable.

DO NOT BE a lesbian. When I was growing up, the word for homosexual in Xhosa was "isitabane". I knew from a very young age that being "isitabane" is very bad and I should not be one. I didn't know anyone who was a lesbian in my town, but there were rumours that there were girls who were trying to act like boys. Conversations about izitabane (plural for isitabene) would take a violent turn with my uncles competing over who would have the best punishment if their future child ever turned out to be one. My youngest uncle would always shut the conversation down with "I would stab him". There would be no coming back from that, he won! A child, a knife, a father, a gay, and boom…death.

Church introduced me to homosexuality as a big sin, an abomination. The story of Sodom and Gomorrah were told as a story of how God would punish homosexuals. I became familiar with all the bible verses that clearly stated that being a homosexual was a sin. Homosexuals were not going to partake in the kingdom of God and I desperately wanted to partake. It's funny but also not that my first female attractions were in church. Some of my female friendships were so intense that I knew the platonic line had been crossed, at least by me. My alone prayers at fifteen years old were me begging God to not make me a homosexual. They didn't work because here I am, twenty years later, writing about being a traveling homosexual.

DO NOT BE so black. I was seven years old when Nelson Mandela and his gang were released from prison. I remember protesting around Cala with my uncles those "final" years of the apartheid era, but it wasn't until high school that I really grasped how difficult it was to be black in South Africa. There was an anger and frustration that was visibly present when my history teachers taught South African history. You could *feel* that they had lived through it. Being black in South Africa meant that you had to behave in ways that are acceptable to your white counterparts. You knew from a young age, they would be your future employers. You were encouraged to speak "proper" English, not with that Xhosa accent; it's not nice. English spoken with a "lighter" tone made you sound educated. At church, we prayed in English, conversed in English; English is the language of the smart.

At school, black children were told to either relax or shave their hair but in no way were they to show up with that kinky hair. This is *still* practiced today by the way. We are taught that there is not much beauty in being black especially in our hair. I relaxed my hair for years! I relaxed my hair for so long that the scabs on my sculp just became part of the process, I expected them and found nothing wrong with a bit of sculp burn. Sick.

The white supremacist standard of beauty is continuously perpetuated by us – black people. It shows its ugly horns as colourism, the idea that light skinned black people are more attractive than darker skinned black people. I have to confess that I subscribed to this fuckedupness until I was in my late twenties, and I saw a beautiful Kenyan woman whose skin was a perfect shade of black, dark chocolate with no patches. I know, it didn't have to take this goddess for me to see beauty in all shades of black, but I too am a work in progress.

DO NOT BE a *bad* woman. I am from a family that believes and upholds the standard of the good woman, the dignified woman, the respected woman, the enduring woman, the self-sufficient woman and yes, the strong woman. We all learn to be this woman when we are girls. My grandmother is the best woman I know. She also made sure that she would, against all odds, raise other good women. What defines a good woman in my family is perseverance, strength, and an unshakable belief in God. A good woman is one who perseveres in marriage. She shows strength in difficult times and believes that God cannot give you more than you can handle. She has her shit together, especially in public.

Good women get married to men and have children. They raise their young in the ways of the Lord and do not air their laundry in public. I was already cooking at eight years old, doing everyone's laundry at ten and helping my grandmother at the prison where she cooked for prisoners. I was frequently reminded that these skills were going to make me a good mother and wife. In hindsight, they have, only to a woman.

I tried as much as I could, as much as anyone could try to deny parts of themselves. I reasoned and bargained with God to make me a heterosexual. I threw myself to all things church. I found a boy I thought I would marry. He was wonderful but not for me. I tried and I failed. I failed at being socialized. The conditioning of how someone with this body and, this skin colour is supposed to be became too great of a burden to bare.

The more I tried, the more I failed, and that failure led to shame and deep depression. There is no faking joy when we are not being the true expressions of ourselves. Joy comes from living authentically. Any moment of happiness that comes when we are in hiding is a temporary fix. What sustainable joy can one have when they are in shame and hiding eighty percent of the time? The other twenty percent is those stolen moments of pleasure, I will be sharing those moments with you in the chapters to come. I lived like this until a friend of mine presented me a different option, one a girl from the small town of Cala could never have fathomed. An option that I thought only possible in my dreams and fantasies.

4

When the option was presented to me; I jumped to it, heart first and head later. The option was to travel. Well, not to travel at first but to go work as an English teacher in South Korea. This is where it all began. This is where I fell madly and deeply in love with this black, queer woman. Travel saved me, it reintroduced me to myself and facilitated the first move towards self-love and self-acceptance.

This story is one of triumph, the daring to be oneself in a world that deems you unlovable. It is about love, heartbreak, loss, and more love. The story is continuous, the journey to becoming never ends, but in this book, I share with you what has already transpired. I pray that you are inspired, and you too find the joy in your own personal journey.

Chapter 1

The Place I call Home

I am from a small town called Cala in the Eastern Cape, South Africa. The town is so small that many South Africans do not even know it exists. We comfortably share our one main road with cows and the occasional goat. Our street corners are buzzing with shoe repair stores that play loud gospel music and young boys who forcefully ask you for 2 Rands at the entrance of the three major grocery stores. I vividly remember the year the town got electricity; I was excited to have my books not covered in candle wax anymore. I knew not to use the paraffin lamp for my homework because it was expensive, and candles were cheaper. Sometimes I got yelled at for not doing my homework when it was still light outside in order to preserve the candles.

I would be reprimanded for caring too much about friends instead of schoolwork. My mother hated friends, and thought they were the root of all evil. I did not even have a lot of friends though; I was a visibly poor child. My school shoes had different color threads from being fixed too much, my one school shirt was yellowed with a few buttons missing and a rip on the collar. My worn-out uniform was the reason the boy I liked made fun of me in front of our schoolmates. A friend told him I thought he was cute, and he looked me up and down, laughed and pointed at the missing shirt button that made my tie look clumsy.

"Andinoze ndijole nalento mna," he said. (I would never date that thing.)

I was used to being laughed at by kids at this point. In primary school, everyone laughed at me at for being a shepherd girl. That is when I started milking my father's cows. I would sometimes show up to school covered in cow fur or forget to take off the shorts I wore while milking the cows and just throw my school dress over them. Kids are mean. I was resilient as fuck though; I entered beauty pageants knowing that I would lose. I was happy with the handkerchiefs they gave to the losers.

Cala was not always unkind to me. I had the best English teacher in primary, Sir Duna. This man taught me that doing anything without passion is pointless. He taught English with the same level of passion that he had when he conducted the school choir. He was my neighbor and I loved walking to school with him in the morning. He was tall, big and loud. He did not walk, he glided. I had to jog to keep up with him. He would tell me how smart I was during these walks. He forced me to only speak with him in English.

I also had the cows. They were my best friends. I learnt how to whistle in a way that would make them obey me. Each cow had its own personality; Mistress was shy and submissive. I could milk her without tying her back legs. Then there was Romaise, oh she was a meanie! She once chased me around the house. I ran and ran but she chased and chased me until I gave up, leaned against the wall and she pinned me between her horns. She would have stabbed me had I been a few kilos bigger. I cried for hours — not because Romaise was mean, I knew that about her — it is that she was mean to me! After all the hours, I'd spent walking her to the grazing fields before school, bringing her back every evening and defending her from dogs, she tried to hurt me. My mother said it was because one of the shirts from the laundry I was carrying was red. She explained that Romaise associated red with challenge and instructed that I never wear red shirts when I'm around the cows again. I listened.

I owe my sense of fortitude to Cala. This town either makes or breaks you and I dare say that it made me.

When I was trying to be cool, I'd tell people that I was from Queenstown. Queenstown was the nearest big town from mine — only an hour away or forty-five minutes if you were a fast and furious driver like my aunt. This was the town that would be flooded on payday with people from the surrounding smaller towns and villages. When I was a little girl, I had "isixhobo" — a tooth that was growing on top of my other tooth. My mother promised to take me to Queenstown to have it removed and I waited over four months to get an appointment date. I would finally see the magical town. The Queen's town.

Three days before my dentist appointment, I was playing with my eight-month-old nephew. I was throwing him up in the air, when his tiny feet hit my mouth – sending the unwanted tooth to the back of my throat while crushing my dream of going to Queenstown with it. That kick didn't hurt as much as the tooth that was already loose, but the sound of the kick sent me screaming and I dropped that baby on the ground as if he knew what he was doing. I was a few seconds short of kicking him back on his tiny baby mouth.

I could feel the sense of relief wash over my mother as her salary as a prison cook would not have afforded that trip. I was devastated, not only because I was eager to see Queenstown, but my mother had promised to take me to KFC after the dentist's appointment. My neighbor's father was a school principal, and he would make those Queenstown trips regularly. I would know he had gone because my friend's school lunch would have a perfectly golden fried piece of chicken – which she said was KFC – but would not share. I used to envy her, her shirt always crispy white, her shoes shiny and socks without holes on the big toe and she would get KFC once every month. Such luck in life.

My parents could not afford the luxuries afforded by school principals and nurses. My neighbors were all rich, well, that is what I thought; teachers, nurses and police officers made a lot of money. We were one of the two households in my street that were poor. We had the school principal who was married to a nurse on our left, the director of a Non-Governmental Organization who was married to an education inspector to our right, the lawyer married to a nurse opposite, the other houses had a lot of teachers, and at the corner was the old lady who was a traditional healer. We used to go to the traditional healer when we ran out of sugar or salt, and they would come to us when they needed something.

My father was an unpaid priest and homemaker. He made his financial contribution with his monthly government pension. I slept in the same bed with them and when he would receive his check, he would buy a big piece of fish which the three of us would enjoy before going to sleep. He would also save some money for me to have milk so when the rest of the family was having their "umphokoqo" known as krummelpap in English, with sugar water, I would have mine with milk. Krummelpap is made with maize meal which is powdered corn and is paired with fresh milk, or sour milk. If there was no food at the house, I would go to the police station to eat whatever my mother had cooked for the prisoners that day. I remember being poor, wanting things that I knew we could never afford but I don't remember ever being hungry. The prison cook and poor priest made sure I was fed.

My father died when I was nine years old – he was seventy-two years old. He had been so excited to finally vote the weeks leading up to his death, and my sisters spent weeks teaching him what to look for on the ballot paper and how to draw his X. Black South Africans only got their right to vote in 1994. Before that, racist white men were appointed by racist government officials to represent black communities in parliament. 1994 was a milestone for black South Africans and my father was beyond himself with excitement. I can imagine being alive for so long, seeing white people exercise this right that affects your life and not have a say on who gets elected and then to finally have that right in your 70s!

"You should look for the spear and shield dad, next to it will be Nelson Mandela's face, then put your X inside the box," my sisters excitedly instructed him.

When the day finally came, he left the house at 4 a.m. trying to make sure he was one of the first in line, but he ended up waiting for six hours. He then came home, asked for a cup of tea, went to his garden and that is where he died.

My father battled asthma for years and on that day, April 27 of 1994, it killed him. I was nine years old when I watched the best man I ever knew and would probably ever know take his last breath on earth; his arms stretched out like he was hanging on a cross. How significant, for a priest to die emulating the symbol of the cross. This day that was supposed to be a celebratory moment ended up being the worst day in our lives. The doctors said that he got so excited that his asthma reacted; I take comfort in knowing that he died in extreme excitement. Like, he overdosed on life's ecstasy.

"Khanyisa ngen'endlini" (Khanyisa get in the house), the older people screamed at me in panic when they finally realized I was standing over my father's dead body.

He did not say goodbye to me, how I wish he did. How I wish he sat me down and taught me how to fend for myself when he goes and never comes back. I wish he had told me that he will not be there when I come home from school, and I would have to learn to make my own lunch. He could have told me that though those men were his sons, they were nothing like him. He could have better prepared me for what was to come after he left.

After my father died, I began doing some serious chores. The first time I cooked was a hot mess! I was told to make umngqusho; it is a traditional African dish made of samp (corn) and beans. It takes hours to cook; you just boil it and keep adding water until its soft, add cooking oil and salt and then viola! Dinner is served. Sounds easy, right? Wrong! Not when you are cooking for a household of over ten people, and you are ten years old. The pot was too big for me to carry off the flaming stove. My meal was done cooking and I had to take it off, but I could not. I dropped it and everything was on the unwashed and unswept floor.

However, the gods were on my side; there was no one in the house! What are the chances of that happening!? I had to decide; throw it away or put it back in the pot. I chose the latter. I took a spoon, got on my knees, and put every grain of samp and beans back in that pot. I went to the tap outside, washed it, reboiled it a little bit and then served it to the people.

"Indala intombi ngoku, iyakwazi nopheka" (The girl is old now, she can even cook) mother said with such pride in her voice.

I did not feel guilty that day, I felt useful. Growing up in a house where people have no problem of calling you a "donkey" would do that to you. Any form of praise is acceptable regardless of what you did to get it.

"Khanyisa wake up, it's six o'clock now, you need to milk the cows and send them to the field to graze," my mother said one morning.

"I need to do what?!" I thought to myself.

"Your brothers have decided that it's time you learnt how to milk a cow, they refuse to do it and all the milk goes to waste," she continued.

My brothers began to undermine my mother's authority when her husband died. She was a woman and that gave them authority over her, forgetting that it was her vagina that pushed them out and her hard work that gave them the very bed they were refusing to get out of.

11

My cousins used to visit us during school breaks, city kids that wanted to learn the ways of the villagers. They would want to learn how to milk a cow and would want to tag along with my brothers when they went to fetch the cows from grazing. I would get caught up in the excitement of doing all these things and had no idea that there would come a day when I would be expected to do them.

My mother had no doubt in her mind that I knew how to milk a cow when she woke me up that morning. She had seen me do it! I despised my city cousins; their curiosity put me in that position. I woke up and furiously milked every single drop of milk that cow had.

If only I had been bold enough to say:

"No, I am a girl, girls don't milk cows they only drink the milk. Girls play with dolls and wear pretty dresses. Now, look, I have accepted that we were bouncing on the poor side of things, and I do not have things those other girls have. But, you are pushing it if you think I'm going to sit on an old paint tin and milk a cow when this house is full of men who'll be sleeping while I do it."

I did not say that, in fact I faked enjoying milking the cow because if I had opened my mouth, my mother would have beat the crap out of me. That woman was the most creative punisher I have ever known. She once tied a rock on a scarf and used it to beat my brother because he was refusing to go to school. Not only would she hit you, but she'd be talking while she is doing it. She would give you physical and emotional pain at the same time. I would listen to my friends talk about how they prefer being hit over being yelled at; I had no choice.

Needless to say, in a few weeks I was whistling, walking up and down the mountain like a real shepherd boy, oh I mean girl. Before I knew it, the cows and field were my sanctuary. It was far away which meant no one could reach me and that also meant that no one could hurt me. I will never forgive the person who decided to steal all our cows, he did not only steal them, but he also stole my hiding place and my best friends. I was left alone, well, with the brothers and my mother but I felt alone.

When I was thirteen, one of my sisters, Margaret asked me to visit her and her family in Queenstown. Finally!!! I was going to Queenstown and not just a day trip, but I was going to stay with them for three weeks. Excited is an understatement. I was elated! My dream of walking those Queenstown streets was going to come true. No more imagining what Queenstown looks like, now more wondering what KFC smells like, I was going to see it with my own eyes. The last week of school before the holidays was too long; I told anyone who'd listen that I was going to Queenstown. Not only was I going, but I was going to stay there for a whole three weeks.

The day finally came, my mother took me to the bus stop and told me to be good. She didn't need to tell me that, I knew what happens when you're bad, so I knew I would be good. My sister's husband, Rhura, picked me up from the bus stop in a police van. I always liked my sister's husband. He was tall, light skinned, and always had his hair in perfect curls. He liked me too, he would always call me "his girl". When him and my sister would visit us during Christmas, he would make sure I knew he paid for the bag of Christmas clothes.

Rhura and I drove through the streets of Queenstown and man – it did not disappoint. All the roads were paved, the streets were clean and all the stores I would see advertised on TV were in Queenstown. I fell in love with Queenstown. Queenstown felt like a city to me. The streets were busy but not loud. There were no cows in site on the main roads, only fruit stands, but nice and well-organized fruit stands. Not like the ones we have in Cala with torn tablecloths and some with rotten fruit on display. There were also white people walking around the street in Queenstown, they looked like they lived there.

The drive to the house was not too long, it was a quick ten minutes from the bus station. I was greeted by my sister, tall, dark with the best teeth in the family even with the two gaps in her mouth. Her smile made things feel better. She was hands down my favorite sister. This was the longest time I spent with her. Before this, I'd only see her during short Christmas visits and a few weekends. Her visits always made me so happy. She laughed like someone had told her not to and she was rebelling. Her laugh was loud, uncontrollable, and unrestricted. My nephews were also there, all three of them - Bonga, Gimba and Ntuntu. Bonga was only a year younger than me and most of the three weeks was spend trying to outdo him at everything!

We spent the three weeks of my school holiday together and I did not want to go back to Cala. I was thirteen years old but already knew how to do most of the housework. I did most of the cleaning during the week and on Saturdays we would do the laundry together. It was during our laundry washing time when she asked.

"Do you know who your mother is?"

I had always thought that the prison cook, and the priest were too old to be my parents even though I thought of myself as their last born. Our cultural practice – as Xhosas, is that a child born outside of marriage belongs to her mother's family and is the grandparents' responsibility. That puts the burden of raising the child on the mother and her family, and completely ignores the fact that it takes two to tango. I am such a child, one of my "brothers" used to get drunk and call me "umgqakhwe" which I later learnt means "bastard child". He would walk in the house, tumbling and yell "yeh wena mqgakhwe,yiza nokutya kwam" (Hey you bastard child, bring me my food).

No one sat me down to tell me that the prison cook and the priest were my parents; it just felt like they were. They raised me like I was theirs. My grandfather used to yell at my "sister" when she'd try to discipline me.

"Andinamntana ozoqeqesha omnye apha," he'd say. (I don't have a child that disciplines another here.)

14

We were both seated on the edge of the bathtub hand washing everyone's clothes when my sister asked me if I knew the family secret. My heart began to race, I was scared. I thought she found out that I knew, and I was in trouble. This is one of those secrets that anyone who dared danced around received the fiery flames of my mother's rage. Anyone who ever mentioned that I was not her child would be sent to hell and back. I couldn't be one of the people who "knew". So, when my sister asked, I fidgeted, shifted from her, broke eye contact and hoped that she couldn't hear how loud my heart was beating.

"Yes, it's Kuku." I replied acting confused.

Kuku is what I called my mother even though my brothers and sisters called her mama. I called my father "tat'omkhulu" (grandfather); it's what my nieces and nephews called them, and they were around my age. Apparently, my eldest nephew couldn't pronounce Makhulu (Grandmother) so he called her Kuku and it stuck. They never corrected me but would always make sure that I knew *they* were my parents. My mother would say she has nine children, and I was her last born.

"Lisana lam eli, liphuma aph'a kum ebeleni" (this is my baby, she nursed on my breasts), she'd say whenever she talks about me to other people.

"No, I am your mother." Margaret said smiling.

I had always known that she was my mother. Some people in my town would make comments about it but I knew for certain when my mother and I went to Elliot to apply for my birth certificate. I was about ten years old and needed to have a birth certificate for school. Elliot is a small town, only a thirty-minute drive from Cala but it was nicer. The streets were paved, and they had electricity. I think it's because the town had a lot of white people, even the white shop owners in Cala lived in Elliot. The home affairs in Cala didn't process birth certificates and we had to plan a trip to Elliot. My mother was asked to fill in a form but because she couldn't read English, the lady did it for her and asked her the questions.

Although Afrikaner, the home affairs lady spoke fluent Xhosa, she asked all the questions in Xhosa but switched to Afrikaans for the question to which the reply was "1966". My "sister" was born in 1966, and hearing that, I knew exactly what the question was.

"Do you know who your father is?" my sister continued her quest to what I knew about my parents.

Now this question shook me. Who else would it be but the man she was married to, who was always nice to me and made me feel like I was his?

"Ewe, ngutata ka Boss." (Yes, Boss's father.)

Boss is my nephew Bonga's nickname, he used to say he is the boss of the house and we just started calling him "boss".

"No, it's a man named Sonwabo Madolo, do you know him?" Frozen in time I did not reply, I just stared at her.

The Madolos went to the church that my father was a priest at. I knew the granny very well, we used to go to her house to eat her blackberries when they were in season and sometimes the church service would be at her house. I would also go to her house during school vacation to play with her grandchildren when they were visiting from Johannesburg.

"Well, he is your father, and he has asked to meet you."

What an adventurous three weeks. I had finally gone to Queenstown, was let in on the big family secret - that my sister was my mother, my nephews were my brothers, and I had a father who wanted to meet me. Not only that, but my sister – who is now my mother, asked my mother – who is now my grandmother, if I could live with her in Queenstown the following year. I felt new in those three weeks, like my life had changed. My sister asked me to stop calling her "sisi" and call her "mama" because "she gave birth to me". I loved that! She was the appropriate age to be my mother. She also let me drink Coca-Cola with the grownups, something Kuku would never allow.

Kuku was pissed off when she first heard me call my sister Mama the first time. "I'm sure utata is turning in his grave right now! You are my child, not hers. I am your mother". She called my grandfather Tata, although husband and wife, she gave him the type of respect one gives her father. You could see it in the way she talked to him, waited for him to take the lead in every decision and when month end came, she submissively gave him her paycheck. I've never seen them kiss or even hold hands, but I've also never seen them fight or raise their voices at each other. She still brags about how he never hit her and how they never went to bed angry. What a privilege for a woman to not be hit by her husband. I'm sure his friends called him a softie. Men are taught to infanticide their wives, treat and discipline them in the same way they do their children.

I was worried that Kuku would say "hell no" to me attending high school in Queenstown. But to my surprise, she agreed. The next year couldn't come fast enough. Before that though, I was to meet this man who was my father, this stranger who I was told I am a splitting image of. Kuku refused to have that meeting take place in her house, so we met at my aunt's – my previous older sibling's - house. She was not okay with what was happening and was convinced that my grandfather would feel the same way as her. The pair of them never forgave him for denying I was his child.

"Ohh, ndilichubile itapile ngoku bayilifuna." (I've peeled the potato now they want it.) She would often say with a disgusted frown. I was of course the potato, her masterpiece.

Sonwabo pulled up at my aunt's house in a red BMW with tinted windows. Kuku had warned me about men in cars with tinted windows, she said they were murderers, and their windows are tinted because they didn't want the police to see them. She said if I wanted to die, I should get in a car with tinted windows. But Sonwabo, walked out of that car with a huge smile on his face, spread out his arms and said, "Come here baby." This was a hug, my first hug from a man, a stranger who was also my father. "Yiya kuye Khanyisa." (Go to him Khanyisa.) My aunt encouraged, and I made my way to that hug. It was warm and it felt safe. It felt like getting something I had been missing but did not know I was. My brothers – who were now my uncles - were abusive in every sense of the word, if they weren't yelling, they were hitting, if they were not hitting, they were molesting.

Part of asserting their dominance as men of the house, my uncles also took it upon themselves to be my disciplinaries. My grandfather never allowed them to hit me; like he would say, he disciplines his children. He never hit me, not ever. Kuku did all the punishing. He also never told her when I misbehaved; she would have to see it for herself. However, after he died, that all changed. I don't remember the first time they hit me; it just became so constant that I don't even know when it began. My uncle, the youngest of the bunch had the shortest temper and majority of the beatings came from him. He would take a wet kitchen towel and hit me with it on my butt. Shit that hurt! He didn't have to have a real reason to hurt you like that; anything would make him hurt you, from a broken glass to a slow walk when he called you. He was always ready to punish.

I do remember when the beating progressed to sexual molestation. There was a family event which had distant family members from outside spending a long weekend at our house. One of the uncles, John, was the first person to touch me. He pipped his head out of the window to call out my name as I was playing with my cousins. I was ten years old. He asked me to climb into bed with him and thus began the humping, the sweating, more humping and then it stopped. It felt like time stood still, it felt like someone had robbed me. I did not know what they took but it felt like they took something precious, something I wasn't ready to give.

"Ungaxeleli mntu uyeva, uzobasengxakini" (Don't tell anyone okay, you'll be in trouble.)

How would I even say it, who would I say it to, what would I tell them happened? "Uncle John breathed and sweated on top of me". My grandmother would pinch me and tell me I did something wrong. What happened felt wrong, being asked to keep quiet about it affirmed that it was wrong. I don't remember what I did after that but knowing me; I probably went back to play with the other kids and pretended like nothing happened. I did have a feeling that something inside me had changed. I had changed. Not only had I changed, I was also not safe. I lived in a house with men who beat me and sexually molested me.

So, when I hugged Sonwabo I knew what an unsafe touch from a man felt like and his was nothing like what I knew. It was kind, not scary, but rather comforting but most importantly, it was in public. His hug said, "I am so happy to see you, you are in loving arms, you will be okay". I needed that hug.

Meeting my father was not an easy journey, it was filled with confusion and painful change. My stepfather who used to love me began to loath me. Rhura was my first lesson in love. He taught me how swiftly love can turn to hate. He showed me what the meaning of "he has changed" truly is, I carried this lesson with me forever, I know that people who love me, can decide to unlove me. Rhura taught me that love is wavering, it is not set in stone and definitely not infinite. I have an incomplete infinity tattoo sign on my arm, it reminds me that nothing is permanent, things change, and people change their minds about you. Rhura taught me this, the hard way.

When I moved to Queenstown, the six of us lived in a garage at the back of someone's house. My two brothers and I shared the pullout couch while the youngest slept with the parents. We would take turns sleeping with my mother when Rhura worked overnight duty. He was a police officer and a drunk. Rhura never hit me, not once, not even when he was at his drunkest. But what he did was worse; he broke my spirit. He made me feel unloved, unwanted and in the wrong place. He made me know that I did not belong there; and I was a huge inconvenience.

He used words and when they failed him, he used other measures. He once put me in the back of his police van, drove fast around town while he teargassed me. I can still smell the teargas. I had no idea what it was, but I cried and begged him to stop. I was sure that I was going to die, either the fast driving or the inability to breathe was going to kill me. It was those tin teargasses, not enough to kill you but enough to make you think it can. When he finally stopped and brought me home, I couldn't stop crying and shaking. I threw up and my throat burned for days. My mother reprimanded him, and then made him dinner. She loved him. She loved him in ways that he did not deserve to be loved. She loved him to a fault, like, loving him was the only things she knew how to do well. It was the "I'll choose you over anything, including myself" type of love. He knew that she loved him like this and he did everything knowing she would always love him just like this.

Rhura is also the only person who has ever pulled a gun on me – this was a regular occurrence. I almost soiled myself the first time it happened. He came home around midnight, drunk and pissed off. He was always angry at something when he was drunk. It was only a matter of who would be at the mercy of his rage. This night, it was me, again. He was angry that he had a child that wasn't his at his house. "Idikazi" (a whore child), that's what he would call me when they were fighting. That night, he didn't even start a fight with my mom, he just walked in and waved his gun at my face. He said "I could kill you". I didn't move, I clung to the blanket real tight, prayed that it would somehow stop the bullet should he shoot. He didn't, instead, he went to bed, woke up that morning and went to work.

20

My life became split between school vacations spent at my father's big house in Johannesburg. Johannesburg was nothing like Queenstown. I remember the first time I went to visit. I arrived at 3am and the city was already awake. All I could imagine when I was a little girl was Queenstown, talk about dreaming small. Johannesburg felt like it was the size of ten Queenstowns. The drive from Queenstown to Johannesburg is ten hours. Ten hours of sleeping and waking up to the sound of South African gospel music on the bus. When we arrived in Johannesburg, the first thing I noticed were the city lights. They were beautiful. The Coca-Cola building stood and towered over the city as if it was its watchmen. My heart dropped; fear ensued with pockets of excitement.

My father came to pick me from the biggest station I had ever seen in my life, Park Station. He got out of the car to find my bus and there he was, waiting with that big smile of his when he saw me. When we went to the car, his wife was there, and she turned with her face stone cold and said "sawubona' (hello in Zulu) and looked away. No smile, nothing. Then, the tension settled in, the car became cold like an ice box, and I thought "shit, she doesn't want me here either". She didn't have to say it; it was all in her silence and the way she greeted me. We drove, the four us; my dad, stepmother, me, and the tension that made itself an invited guest into the car. I survived this first visit and from then, my visits to Johannesburg became regular.

"Do you love your father, Khanyisa?" my mother asked when I returned from one of the school holidays.

"I don't know." I said, caught off guard.

"I want you to love him, if I die, he is the only person that can take of you," she looked serious.

"Okay, I will love him, but you are not going to die," I replied with the naivety of a child.

It was later that same year that my mother was diagnosed with pneumonia and died within a week of her hospitalization. My mother got sick earlier that year. We thought it was a flu, but it just didn't go away. She began to lose heaps of weight and started missing weeks of work. She also became increasingly agitated by me; every small mistake I made would send her to rage. She yelled at everything which was so unlike her. Bonga, my brother noticed this rage and mastered the courage to ask.

"Haybo mama, kutheni soloko umngxolisa kangaka uKhanyisa" (Mom, why are you always yelling at Khanyisa?).

"I want her to be strong, I want her to know how to take care of herself and to be independent." She said;

The shock of being asked made her apologize.

"Uxolo mntanam, ndifuna ukwazi uzimela" (I'm sorry my baby, I just want you to know how to stand on your own).

The yelling stopped after that, but her health did not improve. She went from a big woman; big in every way – big laugh, big heart, big smile, to a small and frail woman.

I was doing my last year of high school and in the middle of my mid-term exams is when she died. I felt abandoned, hung out to dry, sharing space with a drunk who hated me. The church pastor said she told him that she was ready to die when he went to visit two days before she died. I couldn't understand that; how is a woman with four young children ready to die? Why was this man telling church people that my thirty-seven-year-old mother said she was ready to die? Why would she tell him and not me? Being in church taught me not to question the will of God; so when she died, it was the will of God. To mourn (publicly) and to show hurt, would be going against the will of God.

The next year, my father asked that I go live with him and his family to repeat Grade 12 so I could improve my grades and get into university. Life had softened Kuku at that point, she did not put up a fight and actually encouraged the move. Going to Johannesburg for a year was taking care of my future for her. My stepfather's dream for me was to find a job and help him financially. Kuku would rather have me live with Sonwabo; the man she told to go apologize at my grandfather's grave when he asked her for forgiveness, than not go to university.

The most difficult part about leaving Queenstown was leaving my three brothers behind. The experience of losing our mother had brought us close, we had a shared pain. We would say "I love you" to each other almost every day, this hasn't stopped. Our calls always end with "Ndikuthanda nje ngestaring sithanda abantwana baso eTv-ini." (I love you the way the main actor loves his kids in a movie.) We had become a wall of protection for each other. When their father would be a dick to me, they'd all come sit with me in the room and we would pretend he wasn't there.

I had to leave though; my future demanded that I do. I was sure that if I stayed in Queenstown, I'd spend my life working as a secretary or at a retail store. My mother spoke about my graduation way too often for me to not graduate. She was going to wear a yellow suit and a very big hat, that was her dream for me, it was also a dream for my grandmother. They wanted me to be a lawyer, Kuku loved "amagqwetha" (lawyers). I think this is why she put up such a fight for me to go to University, she just wanted to say:

"Ligqwetha uKhanyisa." (Khanyisa is a lawyer.) I was going to be her bragging right.

My first three months in Johannesburg were challenging. On top of it being a massive city, I was living with a woman who let me know that me being there was a favor to my father.

"Culturally, you shouldn't even be here. I am doing my husband a favor by agreeing to you staying with us," she said.

I wasn't sure if I was to thank her, so I just kept quiet as she proceeded to tell me how she felt about me.

"I don't hate you; I don't love you, I am indifferent," she said.

That's where I learnt the word "indifferent". It is when someone doesn't care if you live or die. Your existence has no significance to them. Indifference is the direct opposite of love, not hate like most people believe.

But I didn't just survive that year and her indifference, I thrived. I graduated top of my class with two distinctions. I didn't really have friends in Joburg, all I did was study and play with my little sister. She is the youngest of the three of us and she was my joy in that house. She seemed to instinctively know when I was feeling down and would find a way to make me happy. She was only seven years old but had an opinion about everything. She once asked my father:
"Why do you have to be treated like a king? You just come home, and everyone gives you everything! I don't understand this."
Baffled, my father replied, "because I am the head of this home."

What a grown-up response for a child. This is my culture, the male person who gets waited on every day, everyone's world orbits around him and only when he is satisfied can we all go back to living for ourselves. Women are the carriers of this burden; loving men who do not have the ability or know how to love them back. Women are in service of this man; cooking for him, cleaning up after him and ready to forgive any transgression no matter how deep.

Chapter 2

The Mother City

I have been to a lot of cities around the world, and I am yet to see one as beautiful as Cape Town. It is gorgeous! Cape Town sits on the Indian and Atlantic Ocean; the two oceans meet at the Cape Point. Table Mountain majestically towers over the city and wraps itself around it like a warm hug. Seeing how stunning the Cape is, you can almost understand why Dutch settler, Jan Van Riebeek, chose to pretend that it is his home and then, well, then stole it. He was the very first European to set foot on our shores and then setup refreshment stations for ships going East, he made a pitstop, like those truck towns but for ships. Thus, began our plight as black South Africans, the black bodies who would always belong to white masters, Dutch and British.

I arrived in the Mother City in the wee hours of the morning, just like I did in Johannesburg. The same eight-hour bus ride from Queenstown, the same gospel music, and the same anxiety at the pit of my stomach. But something was different, Cape Town had a sense of calm that Johannesburg did not, the streets were not busy and, the bus station was not overcrowded at four in the morning. What the two had in common were those glistening city lights. However, Cape Town is way prettier – you can see I have chosen a city of my loving. Although I arrived at dawn, I knew I was in love, there is a way that the air felt that made me feel at ease. My heart settled, the fear subsided and only excitement remained.

I was in Cape Town to be a student at the University of the Western Cape. When I finally graduated high school with proper grades, I knew I wanted to be in Cape Town. My plan which was also Kuku's plan was to study Law, but I found out that my father hadn't sent my application forms as he had said he would. I then decided to go to the university and apply in person. When I got there, the law faculty was full and although my grades met all their requirements, they could not create space for me. So, I did what everyone else did - applied at the Social Sciences Department. Not only did my father not send my application forms to the university but to add insult to injury, he also did not want to pay for my registration for a BA degree and told me to sit the year out, go back the next year to study law.

Kuku would not hear of it. She had retired from her job of 21 years as a prison cook and her retirement package was only R10,000 (about $1,000 USD). But with that money, she paid the R3000 (approximately $300 USD) I needed to register and sent more money for me to buy everything I needed for my boarding. We all need a Kuku in our lives, a personal super woman, someone who will move heaven and earth for us. Someone who never tires of being in your corner even when it is at a cost to them. My father did come around and started sending me a monthly allowance when he saw I was not backing down.

One of the important things to do when I arrived in Cape Town was to find a Christian community. My friends from Queenstown were a year ahead of me and they had already found a church and an on-campus movement to be a part of, so I just joined theirs. The church was His People Ministries, and the on-campus movement was called Impact. Impact is where I was most active. Within a few months of being part of the group I was already asked to be one of the group leaders. I was exceptionally good at "Christian-ing". I had been a Christian since high school, at fifteen years old, I was already one of the youth leaders, singing in the choir and sometimes, I'd be asked to pray during the big services. I was a seasoned, tongue speaking, demon basting Christian who could quote John 3 vs 16 word for word, I still can.

"For God so loved the world that He gave his only begotten son, so whoever believes in him shall not perish but have everlasting life."

I told you I was good! For me being a Christian was more of a performance. It was proving my worth to the only community I knew. I knew what to do, who to love and who to shun, which verses to quote, how loud to pray and which voice sounded more Christian. I was good! I was a good Christian, not necessarily a good person, that was secondary, I was a good Christian. I was good at masking, showing parts of me that were only deemed worth seeing and praying everything else away. I prayed the gay away, at least I thought I did, until I moved to Cape Town.

I had always been attracted to other girls, why else would I cry so hard during Friday night prayer meetings in Queenstown, asking God to remove "the spirit of homosexuality". I knew I had that spirit because when my best friend snuggled me, I would get butterflies, crazy butterflies. My heart would race, palms sweat and knees shake. She would touch my hand and I'd feel the touch all over my body. Having prayed and being sure that the Lord answered, imagine the discomfort in my spirit when I couldn't stop staring at one of my classmate's voluptuous cleavage. She walked in at that lecturing hall as if she were the most beautiful thing to ever grace its four walls, swung her hips side to side as though she knew they were her best assets. Her tight blue jeans drew her body like a perfect painting and her low sling white top, showing her massive breasts. I could not stop staring at her, fixated, and infatuated. I convinced myself that I was staring at the rose tattoo she had on her left breast.

I began to drop hints to my Christian friends about my desire to be with women and they would laugh or brush it off. Some would offer to be my experiment so that we could keep it all under wraps and no one would know. My friends didn't know that I was not joking – I was truly struggling – but knowing their stand on homosexuality, I struggled in silence. I had all the scriptures against homosexuality memorized and would recite them to myself every time I thought I should just give in.

"Because of this, God gave them over to shameful lusts. Even their women exchanged natural sexual relations for unnatural ones. In the same way the men also abandoned natural relations with women and were inflamed with lust for one another. Men committed shameful acts with other men and received in themselves the due penalty for their error. Furthermore, just as they did not think it worthwhile to retain the knowledge of God, so God gave them over to a depraved mind, so that they do what ought not to be done."
Romans 1 verse 26-28

Remembering these scriptures, surrounding myself with other Christians and being active in Impact helped me for a while. The random boyfriend here and there also helped but was never enough to hold my attention. All this worked until January of 2006, when a girl from Johannesburg joined our group. Her name was Rato. She was beautiful, her hair too long and too straight for a black girl so it made sense when she said her father was mixed-race.

Rato was light skinned with big breasts, and the confidence she wore made her beauty even more attractive. She knew she was beautiful and she smelled as good as she looked. She would throw her head back when she laughed, fully aware that that would attract attention to her. We were all mesmerized by her; the boys wanted to be with her, and the girls wanted to be her, I wanted both. Our friendship blossomed quicker than sunflowers in summer. Rato and I became inseparable. Our sleepovers became frequent; we divided our nights between my on-campus room and her off-campus one.

The more frequent the sleepovers were, the more intimate they were as well. The snuggling turned to light stroking which created an intense sexual tension. Nothing happened beyond this until one night, on a beautiful Cape Town evening, with the stars glistening over the quiet park we were sitting at in Simon's Town. We frequented the quaint town that is nicely tucked on the eastern side of the Cape Peninsula. Simon's Town embodies the struggle of integration and stamps on the hopes of a rainbow nation. Some businesses proudly wave the apartheid flag, with "whites only" still painted on the outside benches. Whereas others fly the new South African flag - it is a perfect metaphor for my relationship with Rato.

Back to the beautiful evening with Rato and I at the park. I had my head on her lap when she asked:

"Do you ever think about kissing me?"

"Yes," I replied knowing that this would be our first kiss.

She gently removed my head from her lap, placed one hand on my cheek and then the other and pressed her lips on mine. We kissed for a while, walked home after, laid in the middle of the road before entering the house and kissed again. I had kissed boys before, but this was the first time that kissing someone felt so right. Every moment was soft and kind, the tongue didn't rush in my mouth like the boys would, it came in when it was its time. My heart pounced with excitement, and I thought "this is it; this is what being kissed feels like". This was the first of what would be many nights kissing Rato.

The kissing progressed to grinding and then fingering. Rato was my first consensual sexual experience, but I was not hers. She knew how to move my hands to parts of her body that made her feel pleasure. She'd grab my hand, and spread my fingers on her clit, rubbing up and down until she got off. It's the same tactic she used to get me to go down on her. Heavy kissing and then, her hand pushed me down to her clit. That shit would never fly today. I can count with one hand the number of times Rato reciprocated. I just assumed that I was taking on the role of a man-that being on top, conquering my woman is all the pleasure I needed to have. I realized much later in life how selfish of a sexual partner Rato was. She was a self-serving human being.

We didn't have to tell each other that this was a secret, we just knew to keep it. We were still highly active in our Christian lives; she was even the worship leader at her church. But as secrets go, I began to feel the weight of the shame of mine. We had to think of ways to make sure that no one suspected anything and me looking very feminine was vital. I started to wear dresses, high heels, and big earrings-but for us to be believed as "just best friends" I couldn't look "like a lesbian". Our three-year relationship – I reluctantly call it that – was mostly me waiting for her to come back on dates with boys, pretended that I was not jealous she had a boyfriend and wondering what hell would feel like, or if I was already there.

We didn't keep the secret for three years. We were caught! People started to comment on our body language, and rumors began to spread. In their "WWJD" vibe, our Christian friends began to worry about our salvation. They organized a meeting where they would voice their concerns and ask us to stop living in sin. We could not stop though. I was in love with her, she was, by definition, my first love. We were stuck in an emotional push and pull for those three years. I was living in shame and felt that she wasn't taking it as seriously as I was. Rato was confident in her belief that there was nothing romantic going on between us; we were just friends who "played" with each other. She told me that she played with all her best friends, even some of the girls in her volleyball team played with each other. It drove me crazy thinking that that's all I was to her, just some toy.

Rato loved being beautiful, she enjoyed thinking that people thought she was the most beautiful girl in the room. She craved the attention she was getting from everyone, especially men who wanted to marry her. She would often ask if I thought she was as beautiful as everyone said she was.

"Do you think I'm very pretty. It's kind of abnormal how many men want me, right?" she'd ask trying to hide the obvious grin.

"Yeah, I think you are," I'd reassure her.

One of her suitors was a famous soccer player in Cape Town. He would pick her up for fancy dates and soccer matches. I vividly remember his small orange car, his straight white teeth that glimmered through his dark skin when he smiled. It was a game night he hosted that ended our "situation-ship".

"I'm tired and want to go home," I said to Rato motioning for the door past midnight.

I was not drinking that night and hanging out with drunk people was not ideal. He motioned for her to go to his bedroom which stayed shut for about thirty minutes when she went in. I sat there slowly sipping on some Coca-Cola, pretending that they were just talking. The drive home was a tense silence from me, ignoring every attempt to include me in the conversation.

"He asked me why you act like my lover." Rato said

"How is me wanting to go home acting like your lover?" I said, preparing to sleep on the floor.

"Oh, you will sleep on the floor now?! You're so dramatic."

I didn't want her near me, she repulsed me that night. I realized that she didn't love me the way I loved her.

"Yep!"

"Oh, FUCK YOU, Khanyisa. We are not lovers!"

I woke up the next morning, called my grandmother to ask her for bus money to go home to Cala. I was mid-packing when Rato woke up, there was no "sorry" strong enough to persuade me to stay. She knew how I felt about people saying "fuck you" to me. I told her about how I didn't speak to a friend for over a week because he had said that to me. It's crazy how with everything that I endured with her, the lies, the pretending, the soul torturing-it took her saying "FUCK YOU", that one time for me to leave. Maybe it's true that it can take one small thing to destroy a relationship. Like Jenga, one small piece can cause the whole thing to come crumbling down.

It was difficult to mourn the end of that relationship in a way that one mourns a breakup. Rato was indeed my first love. I felt things for her that I had never felt for anyone else. I finally understood the soap operas I wasted my evening on when I was in high school, the romantic songs, especially Flying Without Wings by Westlife. I studied her every move; I knew every different smile she had and what each meant. I looked beyond that beautiful face, saw someone with a lot of pain and made it my job to love her through it. I wanted to fix her.

Now I know that it is not my job to fix anyone. I know it is toxic to enter a relationship having a savior complex. I know that people are not broken, and if they are, I cannot fix them, only they can fix themselves. Maybe I was broken, maybe I wanted my broken to meet her broken and be broken together. Maybe I was not broken, maybe I wanted love, love that didn't ask me to hide it, love that was open and free. Or maybe I was just a gay Christian, living in sin and shame and wanted company. Whatever the reason, it was not healthy, and it ended in way that every unhealthy relationship ends…horribly.

The common expectation in South Africa and I guess everywhere in the world is that once you graduate you will get a job. Go to university, graduate, get a good job, in that order. No one prepares you for the daunting experience of looking for a job or at least no one prepared me. I expected it all to be easy and to just fall into place, but I learnt that nothing is easy. "Education is the key to success" is what everyone said. I heard this statement from when I was in grade one all through university. Once you have an education, you are guaranteed success. I thought it was the law, and that law justified all the sleepless nights and the huge debt I was in from my student loans. What these people failed to tell us, including Nelson Mandela by the way, is that finding a job after you graduate can be a nightmare.

My first job after graduating was a call center agent in Cape Town. We would call people and ask them to take out a loan, what surprised me most about that job was how easy people would give you their bank account number. I held it for a whole month, it was a long month of being told to fuck off and getting asked out on dates solely because my voice sounded like I was pretty. I became depressed with living in Cape Town; I was an unemployable graduate, sharing a dorm room with her closeted lesbian lover. I was still calling my family to ask for money even though I was a graduate. Graduates are supposed to have fancy jobs and provide for their families, not the other way around. Black children are expected to take care of their families, it's not a choice, it's an obligation. We judge people who don't send money home every month in support of their parents. We are expected to somehow pay back all those years of being raised as if we asked them to birth us. I felt like such a failure, this was not how I had imagined this graduate experience to be.

I did not disclose to my family about my breakup with Rato, because I would have to disclose about my sexuality, and I was not ready. Instead of letting them in, truly in on what was going on with me, I told them a story they would believe, one they see all the time, the statistic, the story of an unemployed graduate. Finding Khanyisa a job became everyone's mission. My aunt and I personally drove to offices that were hiring to drop off application forms. What I realized, the painful way those few months, is that your qualifications are not that important when looking for government jobs, it is who you know and who that person knows that will get you hired. Being from a poor family in Cala meant that no one knew us and therefore the jobs were not for me.

I finally got a job in Queenstown as a teacher. Yep, I was back in the Queen's town, teaching at the school my church owned. I hated being back in Queenstown that year. I was back to the same crowd, the same people, the same conversation and hiding my sexuality. I had cracked the closet door and experienced being in love with a woman. A few of my friends knew but they assumed I was bisexual, a label much easier to accept as it keeps the option of being heterosexual open. There was no room for such flexibility in Queenstown. I knew I had to get back to what everyone remembered me as; the overly zealous Christian and I wasn't that anymore. I faked it for a while, pretended to pray in tongues and talked about one day having a husband. The town I used to be so enamored with when I was a child became a box so small that I felt claustrophobic. It felt like I was drowning and I needed to get out.

When winter vacation time came, I made my way to Cape Town to visit my best friend, Neli and never went back. I did not even inform the school that I wasn't coming back for two weeks, I did feel bad about leaving them hanging but I was not happy. Watching my mother persevere in her marriage regardless of how unhappy she was made me vow to never do that. I was also an unhappy child and therefore, as an adult I felt I had more control over my happiness and so I told myself, "When you are not happy, leave". This has not been an easy motto to live by, sometimes it takes longer for me to decide to leave but I always eventually do.

Not much had changed in Cape Town; I was still unemployed, still very closeted and still feeling very depressed. The only thing that was different was that I was not talking to Rato, even though she was still in Cape Town. I also had a boyfriend. I know, right? Pain and shame met, led me straight to Leo's arms. He worked with Neli and that is how we met. I think I hit on him, I said: "How is a decent man like you single?" and he said, "maybe I am waiting for a decent woman, like you." That was it, we put our 'decencies" together and became boyfriend and girlfriend.

Leo was a kind, well spoken, Christian boy, just what society ordered. He just looked like he was going to be successful. He was an entry level economist at Deloitte. Leo was perfection, he was dark skinned, straight white teeth, well-kept short hair and kind eyes. However, as an economist, he was stingy as fuck! He once made us share a McDonald's burger on a date. He had a small notebook in his car, in which wrote down every time he bought something, every.single.time. It must be the traits of the job, it might be his character and that's what led him to the job, I don't know. All I know is that I will never go on a date to McDonalds again.

It was nice having a boyfriend, though, the things that are nice about someone claiming you as their own. The public handholding, surprise chocolate and masculine presence. Leo had an acceptable amount of masculinity, strong, assertive with a large dose of kindness. Also, he had a car...don't judge me! I experienced Cape Town through different eyes with Leo. He was spontaneous and would drive to whatever beach we felt like driving to. Never to swim though, no, just to hang out and dip our feet in the ocean. Kissing? Sex?

Kissing, yes, Leo was a virgin when we met and kissed like one too. I wish I had taught him how to kiss me, instead of speaking up, I contended with the sloppy wet drools and faked being happy. We didn't have sex, no. Leo was a good Christian boy who wanted to wait until marriage, that was a perfect set up for me. Even though we lived together for a whole three weeks, Leo and I would have heated make out sessions and exciting dry humps but never intercourse. I wasn't straight, I was conforming to societal norms. Sometimes when he and I kissed, I would stroke his chest wishing for rounder and softer cushions. When we would come close to having sex, my mind would imagine a hot sexy woman.

My last job in Cape Town was a sales rep for a phone company that was going to directly compete with Telcom called Neotel. Telcom has a monopoly in the telecommunications industry in South Africa and Neotel wanted to become its competitor. They promised cheaper call rates and faster internet that ran on fiber optics. We knocked on people's private homes, businesses, and offices convincing people to sign up for this "better internet and phone service provider". It was an exhausting job both physical and emotionally. We got paid on commission which meant no sign ups, no money, so we would fake our client list. A girl's gotta eat!

I did not know the extent of my depression until the night Neli found me crying in her studio apartment. That is when I knew that I was at the peak of my depression. Having a boyfriend was not enough to make me happy, neither was being in my favorite city. It is true, we cannot find happiness outside of ourselves. When we try, we put a huge responsibility on those around us, the responsibility of being our source of joy, and they are doomed to fail. Leo could have been the best boyfriend in the world, and he was in so many ways, I was still very depressed and there was no way of loving me out of that depression. I had to love me out of that depression.

"Nana (Neli and I call each other Nana), what's wrong?" she asked starting to cry.

"I need to get out of this country Nana, I am depressed, and I feel like I need to leave." I said very sure of what needed to happen for me to be happy.

"Let's get you out then," she replied assuring.

Within six months of that conversation, I was on a plane going to teach English in South Korea, where my journey as a travelling black lesbian began.

Chapter 3

안녕하세요!
Anyoung haseyo!

In June 2010, South Africans were World Cup crazy, and I was South Korea crazy. The country spent years and shit loads of money preparing to host one of the biggest sporting events in the world. And I spent months and what was definitely shit loads of money to me as I didn't have any, preparing for the biggest move of my life. I tried to be involved in the excitement but let's face it, I was never a fan of the sports to begin with and plus, all I could think about were my future Korean students, wondering if I will find someone who can do my dreadlocks, and my life in a country that I didn't even know of until I heard that some of my school mates were there teaching English.

I boarded my flight the day after the World Cup started, but not without seeing at least one game. My friends and I watched the very first match, South Africa versus Mexico. We didn't watch it at a big stadium, but a small community field on a massive projector. This was the first time I had seen South Africa like this, so united. Black, White, Indian, Colored and everything in between, we were all there, laying on this well-kept grass, cheering our team on. This must be why Nelson Mandela loved sports the way he did – it was its power to transcend racial lines and bring us all together in a celebratory fashion.

We took our place on the grass next to a White family who adorned each member in the South African team's jersey. We all glanced at each other, smiled, and became one in this moment. Our soccer team, Bafana Bafana gave it their absolute best. We drew; much to my surprise. Let's just say that Bafana Bafana has made a habit out of loosing, which means we celebrated that draw as if it was a win. South Africa is famous in the sporting world for the legendary vuvuzela which I hate.

The vuvuzela is a plastic horn which makes a screeching sound. Soccer players from other parts of the world *actually* petitioned to have the vuvuzela banned as it was too distracting. But the vuvuzela belongs to South Africa and no petition can have it banned in its home. As much as the sound pierced through my ears like a thousand knives, I knew this would probably be the last time I would experience this, and so I asked the white family next to us for their extra one and blew that baby until my lungs began to sting.

Leaving South Africa came with a host of different feelings; I was excited, nervous but also so scared. The fear of the unknown gripped me to the point that some days I would wonder if I was making the right decision. I remember having a mild panic attack when someone asked if I was going to South or North Korea, I had no idea there were two Koreas!

"You better be sure it's not North Korea girl, you won't make it back from there" she said looking worried.

I messaged my agent to confirm I was going to South Korea and their reply was, "We don't send anyone to North Korea." I was not aware of the political structure of where I was going and truthfully, I didn't care, I just wanted to be gone. I was also asked if I wanted to be in a rural area or city. I was not bothered by either of those options plus, I didn't have the time to waste on waiting for an opening in a city or rural area. I wanted both to be viable options for me thus increasing my chances of getting hired.

Another friend warned that I would not want to live in rural Korea and should pray that I get hired by a school in the city. Crazy she warned but had never even been there! It amazes that we so quickly form unwavering opinions about things we have never even experienced. She could have given me a million warnings and I would still not have cared. My soul was ready for the move, I was prepared to push through the fear and start living.

The fear was secondary to the need to live and that made it easier to board the plane when the day came. I wore blue jeans, a long-checkered jacket, and red boots, it was winter in South Africa. I kept that outfit through the duration of the eighteen hour flight. When I arrived in Hong Kong, I walked around the airport pinching myself. It was the only thing I could think of doing in order to bring myself back to reality, I needed to make sure that I was alive because walking around that airport, I felt like I was just floating. I had elevated my level of excitement to the point of feeling numb. It was that point where fear meets excitement, and it dawns on you that you have taken a giant leap and there is no going back.

"This can't be me, the chick from a town that people don't know, is now in Hong Kong."

I burnt all my journals when my mother died, they reminded me too much of her. All the letters I had written to her when she had upset me, the outfit she planned to wear at my graduation which were the exact same outfits she would wear at my wedding and how I felt about her dying. I went to my pastor's wife after the funeral, she is the one who was trusted with the heavy duty of telling my brothers and I that our mom had passed. I told her that I was struggling. I explained that it was becoming unbearable to live in that house without my mother.

"Everything reminds me of her. Her smell still lingers in the house," I told her about a month after my mother died.

She said she had never lost a parent but imagines I needed to be somewhere else, somewhere where I would not be reminded of her. That was difficult since I was still in high school and literary had nowhere else to go. She then pointed me to another church member who lost her father saying, "perhaps she will know what you should do." Looking back at that conversation, I wonder if that was a compassionate and empathetic reply from a "spiritual parent". I have given people sound advice on things I had never gone through before. Pain is a familiar feeling, even if the situations are different. I do not think she meant to be apathetic or dismissive, but it sure felt like she was.

The journals were the only things I could get rid of that reminded me of my mother; and after that meeting, I burnt them to ashes. There would be nothing to remind of how imperfect our relationship was, how there were days that I didn't like her, how she made so many promises she didn't keep - like buying me that cute outfit at Edgars when she got paid. I had everything documented even the way she got angry at small things and how I found that mean.

I stopped journaling after I turned those journals to ash, until this trip, at the airport in Hong Kong. I did not even have a journal, so I bought a notepad at the airport mini mart. I decided to write to Neli in this notepad, it must have been that need to have someone next to us when we go through big changes or even small things like watching your favorite TV show. Everything was so new and pretending that I was talking to her made the journey a little less scary.

"Dear Nana, I've just arrived in Hong Kong. This airport is so beautiful. I just pinched myself really hard to make sure that it was really me here and that I was alive." This is how those entries would go.

When I got off the airplane in Seoul, there was a short Korean man, dressed in a black suit and white shirt; holding a sign that had my name on it. It felt like a movie all he was missing was a huge bouquet and a big smile. I tried to shake his hand for a hello, but he backed off and bowed instead. I know, I did zero research. The sun was not okay with my South African winter outfit. It was scorching hot! Thank God for car air-conditioning, it saved me from passing out from a heat stroke. We drove past the city, passed a few small towns then finally drove inside a school that was surrounded by farms. A group of boys who were playing outside ran to the car followed by another short Korean man who introduced himself as Jun, my co-teacher. The boys were instructed to grab my suitcases and the car that drove me left and it all sank in, "I am here to stay."

"Khanyisa, we were not able to find you accommodation so you will stay at the principal's house here on the school premises." He asked, "Is it okay for you to stay for two weeks while we find you a place in town? I have a few places lined up for you to see, I wanted you to choose the one you liked."

The principal had built himself a nice apartment on the school premises but wasn't living in it. It was more of a storage space but was cleaned out for me to live in it. I couldn't help but think it weird for the principal to be building a house on school grounds when he had a family to go home to after work. It just sounded like something a man that cheats on his wife would do. Jun and I had just met, and I wasn't going to tell him my thoughts, not yet at least.

This was going to be the first time I would have a house that was mine and waiting two weeks for that to happen was not a problem. Although not properly furnished, my intermittent apartment did come with a kitchen, nice little bathroom and a small TV that only played Korean channels. The first night at my new abode was rough. Not only did I have anxiety about sleeping in a new place, but I also forgot to pull the mosquito screens and had the windows open.

I was woken up by what seemed like hundreds of mosquitos and my first thought was "these Korean mosquitos are going to kill me". For some reason, I thought that their bite will be deadlier than the mosquitos at home. I managed to kill all but one. You know that one mosquito that somehow knows you are about to get into a deep sleep and in that moment comes to scream right inside your ear. That sucker kept me up most of the night and had me looking like a zombie for my first day of class.

One of the many things that I did not research about Korea was the food situation. I was not aware of just how different the food would be from what I ate. On the day of my arrival, Jun took me to a restaurant close to the school that he said served ice noodle (냉면).

This is a famous Korean summer dish, a bowl of thin brown noodles swimming in ice and soy sauce. I was to indulge in this summer delicacy using chopsticks! How?! Now, having been raised by my grandmother, I knew that it was rude to turn down food, but I couldn't do it, I just couldn't. My African taste buds were not prepared for those noodles, they were confused by the ice and the sauce was sour.

"It's okay if you don't like the noodles, I'll take you to a burger place in town. You should learn to use chopsticks. That's an important part for living in South Korea," he instructed.

He drove me to the small town; Jeongguk, where most of the other foreign English teachers lived. This is where I would also end up living once I'd found an apartment I liked. Jeongguk, I later found out, it is also few hours from the demilitarized zone famously known as the DMZ line. That is the line that divides North and South Korea. To put it in clear terms, I was way too close to North Korea, close enough to die should they decide to start a war. You can't imagine the terror when news broke of a North Korean military exercise that killed a few people on a nearby South Korean Island.

I asked around about evacuation plans, made sure my name was registered at the South African embassy and limited my weekend trips to Seoul. My fear slowly disappeared when I noticed how sensationalized the whole thing was by the media. It was intriguing to live in a country that was about to "go to war" as per media outlets and sensationalism but watched life go on as normal. I told myself I would start shitting my pants when I don't see the locals on the streets, until then, I would only concern myself with trying to remember my students' names.

The burger place (Lotteria) Jun took me to was buzzing. It became my favorite joint in town; it's where I had my Christmas eve dinner that year. The locals couldn't hide their amazement at what, not who, had just walked in. That was the first time I felt like "a what". I was taller than most of the people, I was bigger and well the obvious, I was black. This town felt like it hadn't seen a single black person in its entire existence. It was at this very same place that a baby, not more than six months old looked at me and screamed. He looked so scared, and the mother looked so embarrassed. The more I smiled at that baby, the louder its cry became. I'm sure that they would say things like "you better finish your food, or the black woman will come". They probably brought me up whenever they wanted that baby to behave. I had never felt as black as I did that day. I truly felt like an anomaly.

Jun had to introduce me to the school principal the next day, a task that he explicitly told me he didn't care for as he wasn't on good terms with the man. Duty called though, he had to put his feelings aside and take me to him. The principal spoke very little English and there would be no conversation between him and I without Jun translating. Another short Korean man, sitting behind a big desk on a big brown leather chair. He got up, came around the desk, stood in front of me and bowed. I was accustomed to the bowing at this point, so I did the same.

"It is very nice to meet you." he said sounding very practiced.

"It's very nice to meet you too." I smiled.

They both started giggling and Jun looked shy.

"He said you are pretty and have a nice smile."

"Thank you."

"I did some research on South Africa." the principal said.

"Oh yeah?" me regretting that I did not do any research about South Korea.

"Yes, did you know that Johannesburg is the same size as Seoul but has fewer people?"

"No, that's very interesting".

"Will you be watching the World Cup?" he asked with excitement.

"Yes." I lied.

And thus, began my career as an ESL teacher, with a lie about watching soccer. One thing that shocked me is how there isn't much difference between South African and South Korean teenagers. They are all the same and I bet they are all the same everywhere. I expected the Korean kids to be more respectful and easier to work with. Nope. Each class had the three class jokers, the group of mean girls, the super smart nerd, the handsome boy, the boys who the other boys wouldn't hangout with and teacher's pet. It was all the same stuff, no different from teaching in South Africa. The only difference is all the kids seemed to look the same. I wasn't being racist; Korea is an extremely uniform country. Not only in the sense that the kids wear uniforms to school, no, but all the girls have long black silky hair with bangs while the boys wear theirs short with bangs. The only boy who was different was the one mixed child in the school. The boys were playing soccer once and Jun said to me.

"Look at the black pig run," he laughed saying that.

He must have noticed the shock and discomfort on my face because he promptly followed with "I'm just joking."

Life was so unfair to that little boy. He was the only black child at the school and on top of that, he was big. Koreans are obsessed with being skinny, pale and enforcing whatever collective idea of beauty they have. Their standard of beauty is measured in relation to Caucasians; whiteness and skinny is the goal. One of the female teachers asked if I knew how Bonga I was for having V-shaped chin and dimples. She told me how badly Korean women want that and how much money they pay to have it. I had already noticed how many Korean women look permanently surprised from having surgery done to make their eyes round. K-pop culture didn't do much to help in affirming natural beauty for Koreans. I learned that most of the K-pop stars have to go through some gruesome grooming at the start of their careers; from surgery to skin bleaching.

My students didn't seem too bothered by the fact that I was black – they were just excited to have a new foreigner teacher. I of course looked like every other famous black person from Beyoncé to Barack Obama. Beyoncé felt like a complement and Obama, well he felt like whatever is in between a complement and an insult. Insulted that they said I look like a man but okay that he was a good-looking man. The boys used to ask me to join their basketball games, because "all black people can play basketball."

I knew nothing about basketball – I am South African, for us it's soccer, rugby, cricket and netball – especially for women. I wanted to be the cool teacher. So, I committed to twice a week basketball games with the naughty boys. It was also my strategy to get them to be my friends to make sure they don't act like assholes in my class. The strategy worked for the most part, except for Kim who was going to be who he was no matter what - an asshole. Kim once gave me the worst fever of my life! Little shitty Kim intentionally sneezed on my face while I was correcting his classwork putting me on bed rest for a good two days. The fury of my colleagues fell so hard on him that he spent a good week apologizing for making me sick.

The only time I had to address racial issues with my students was during my 5th grade class at the elementary school. I was teaching them about animals and when we got to monkey, one boy yelled.

"That's you, teacher." he said it twice with the rest of the class laughing.

It took everything inside of me to not slap that boy across his tiny little face. I walked out at the end of that class and told my supervisor what happened.

"Ha!" exclaimed Jess her face turning red.

She called the homeroom teacher, and the boy was forced to apologize.

"Jess, did you guys explain why it's not okay for him to say what he said?" I asked.

"No, we just told him it's wrong."

"You didn't tell him why it's wrong?"

"No."

Jess picked up where I was going with this line of questioning and then finally told me about how the kids are not their responsibility after school.

"They learn a lot of these things from their parents and there's no way for us to control what they learn at home".

I silently disagreed with this point of view. Having been in Korea for a 2nd year at this point, I knew arguing with authority is the fastest way to lose your job.

I started having a serious love for the nightlife in South Korea. I am an extremely late bloomer; I have my first kiss at eighteen years old and the first time I drank alcohol was my first year in university. Marcy, my friend from Namibia, was not okay with the fact that I'd never drank before. So, one Friday, she decided we were going to have a party and she would teach me how to drink. Boy did we drink! To all their surprise, I was the last man standing. They all forgot to explain to me about what a hangover feels like, I would have opted out of that drinking session had they told me. When I opened my eyes, the ceiling was spinning, and my body refused to get out of bed. I quickly became a seasoned drinker, but all our drinking was done either in our room on campus, the beach or one of our friend's homes. Seoul was a whole new level of drinking.

Neli's friend Mzi, who is now my best friend, took me out to the city my first weekend. He took me to all his favorite spots ending the night with Homo Hill St. The street is named after the fact that it is on a hill and that's where all the gay clubs are lined up. Right next to it is hooker hill, can you guess what goes on there? Yep, that were all the clubs where you can end the night paying well over a thousand dollars for the company of a sexy waitress. This was my first time at a gay club. Rato and I were very closeted, the last place we would want to be spotted at was a gay club. We were not girlfriends, remember, just friends who "played" with each other. Mzi did not know about my past with this girl, the only reason he took me there was to show me where everything was in the city and explained that this is where the most dancing takes place.

Every Christian sermon I had heard about homosexuals came rushing to my mind, I remember thinking, this is what hell must be like; literally. I had the classic case of "internalized homophobia". The club was dark and ridiculously hot. Men were kissing and groping each other. One of the guys had his hand in another guy's asshole and was moving it up and down. I watched in amazement and envy thinking that these people had just allowed themselves to be who they were in a world that I have clearly heard say they were not allowed to exist. It was confusing, this awe and judgement coexisting in my heart.

47

When I saw how progressive Mzi was, I disclosed my sexuality to him, and he was not surprised. We became regulars at the hill. He is openly bisexual. It is his perfect balance of flamboyant and masculinity that makes me love him so much. He is the best wingman any single person can ask for. He is also the best guy to go bra shopping with. I didn't have enough bras when I got to Korea because, they are expensive, and I was broke. Why are they so expensive?! Mzi took me around Itaewon, Seoul watching me get disappointed as most of the shops didn't have my size. My boobs are not big in South Africa, they are average. Imagine my shock when majority of the store owners made "big boob" hand gestures. Mzi walked around that city with me pointing at women's boobs showing me what was considered big, small and average. Let me tell you, Asia is a haven for A-sized women.

I didn't know the deeply ingrained homophobia that is in the minds of Koreans. The more gay friends I made and LGBT-oriented events I attended, the more I was confronted with this homophobia. I was at a point where I could identify the homophobia as hate. I was no longer hiding behind religion; I was part of this community now. I joined a gay affirming church that was led by a gay pastor called Open Doors. The church meetings were held every Sunday afternoon at 3 p.m. in a bar. Sometimes pastor Daniels would have a beer in his hand while he delivered his sermon. It was at this church that I got to see the pain that Korean LGBT go through, the rejection by their families when they come out.

The homophobia became less abstract when one of my best friends was beaten to a pulp by a group of four Korean men who saw him kissing his date outside a bar in Seoul. My friend was brutally attacked and then urinated on because he was kissing another man. The Korean he was kissing got the worst of it. The attackers felt that, as a Korean, he needed to be taught what he was doing was not "the Korean way". They broke his ribs and he spent more than a week in hospital. Many of my friends who dated Koreans would see the relationship end abruptly as soon as the relationship started to get more serious. I thought that was because the Koreans were scared to be seen with the same person and having to explain who they were. Every time I heard such stories, I'd go back to the conversation I had with Jun the Monday morning after my first gay club experience.

48

"How was your weekend, Khanyisa" asked Jun that Monday morning.

"It was great. My friend showed me around Seoul." I replied excitedly.

"Where did he take you?"

"We went to Itaewon and at night we went clubbing, we also went to the gay clubs."

"Gay clubs?! I'm sure there were no Koreans there, there are no gay people in Korea" he said assured.

"Actually, about 80% of people were Koreans and they were gay," I informed him.

"They must have been there for fun not because they're gay."

"No Jun, they were there because they are gay." I told him.

"Korea is a conservative country Khanyisa, being gay is not allowed here."

"That doesn't mean there are no gay people, it just means they are hiding."

This was our first uncomfortable conversation and I had to crack a joke to lighten the mood. I couldn't believe that this grown man genuinely thought that there are no gay people in his country because it's "conservative". As I became more acquainted with South Korea, I began to question what they think of sex and conservatism. There was a statue in the middle of my town that looked like four men in an orgy. They have a park somewhere in Seoul called the penis park. The park is filled with sculptures of erected penises. Whereas, in Jeju Island, there is a love land park dedicated to sex positions; sculptures showing different sex positions. I'm sure people learn new positions that they can take to their bedrooms, kitchens, offices or wherever they have sex. I know there is some deep reasoning behind these parks, but they don't necessary scream conservative but rather the opposite. A friend of mine once said, "They are not conservative; they are sexually confused," I think that makes more sense.

They also have public baths (jimjil bangs), these are naked baths. I must admit that they are amazing, the second time you go, especially if you are black. I was invited by a white girl I had just met and, not a good idea. I still don't know how we went from "it's nice to meet you" to "let's go see each other naked tomorrow" but we did. She had gone already and successfully convinced me that it was the best thing to do. The public baths are divided into two sections; one section is the saunas where men and women can hang out together, then there are the baths, and these are separated.

We started with the saunas easing ourselves to the actual baths. We finally went inside the naked area, and I felt the room become silent; everyone turning to look at us. My first thought was "oh crap I forgot to shave my lady" but looking at the other people's ladies I realized that didn't matter. Korean women do not shave their vaginas. That day I decided there was no way I would ever have sex with them. Korean women. I enjoy going down on women, it's one of the things I look forward to during sex, and I also love a well-groomed vagina. It doesn't have to be bald, or even waxed, just groomed enough for me to not be pulling hair out of my teeth when I'm done. Some of my friends said they'd actually seen Korean women blow dry their pubic hair. That's too much for me!

I was uncomfortable with my new friend seeing me naked and the best way to deal with that was to avoid eye contact at all cost. The baths are big with different pools that have different temperatures, so we just went our separate ways. The Korean women — especially the older women — were much more difficult to avoid. They put very little effort in trying make sure that I didn't see them pointing and talking about me. Some of them even came over to ask to touch my dreadlocks. At some point, I had a posse of women circling me while I showered all asking to touch my dreads. This was not sexy, not even a little bit. You would think that being surrounded by naked women would be a turn on for a lesbian, it wasn't. It was such an invasion of personal space, but I was too polite to let them know I was uncomfortable. I doubt they would have stopped anyway. There was the language barrier, I hadn't learnt "please leave me alone in Korean", I should have.

My hair was such a mystery to Koreans. Once while waiting at the bus stop, I felt what I thought was a bug crawling up the back of my head. I slapped it only to grab the hand of an old, short Korean woman who couldn't resist the urge to touch a stranger's hair. I respectfully lowered my head and let her have her way with it. She touched the tip of my dreads, slowly and carefully investigated them. She took her time feeling the texture with her fingers and then thanked me when she was done. My students used to ask if they could count them and I would sit there, patiently waiting for the little people to count each dread.

One of the things I appreciated about Koreans is their love of hiking and how they make use of their beautiful parks. Each city has a beautiful park where families spend weekends having picnics and couples enjoying each other in nature. Schools would have random days where class would be canceled, buses hired to take teachers and students hiking. Every mountain we hiked would have a lot of Koreans hiking just for fun. I would feel like a celebrity on these trips as fellow hikers would stop me to ask for a picture. I found out that some of my friends hated this but not I, I understood that I was something they had never seen, and I was okay posing for them. I didn't think of it as racist at all. I saw it as an expression of their curiosity and awe of this glorious melanin I am working with.

Growing up in a country where you are not afraid to roam around nature was something new to me. South African kids do not have the luxury of hiking and exploring nature because of the potential harm, a hike could turn into a rape or even murder especially if you are a girl. They kill women, and children in South Africa. I know that sounds a little too farfetched, but it's true. Being a woman in South Africa is a death sentence, it feels like having a ticking time bomb or being in a land mine. There is a femicide going on in my country and the government has refused to address it as such, so women and children keep dying. They are dying at home, at the clubs, in taxi ranks and most recently, the post office. As a woman, you breathe a sigh of relief when you make it from your house to the store and back alive, imagine what being up on a mountain would feel like.

I have to credit that first year in Korea for the person that I am now. When I arrived that year, I was still a closeted lesbian. I was wearing dresses and big earrings even though I hated them. I had become comfortable in pretending to be someone I was not. It wasn't until someone said:

"You know you can be whoever you want to be now. That is the beauty of traveling, you get to reinvent yourself."

A light bulb came on when I heard that; that person did not know that I just wanted to be me. I wasn't going to reinvent myself; I was going to allow myself to be seen. I watched all seasons of "the L word", a Lesbian American TV that became popular among lesbians and "straight women". After the first few episodes, I decided I was Shane. Shane, the sexy hairdresser, who could turn straight women gay and get any girl she wanted – don't bring your girlfriend around Shane. I put all the dresses away; took off the big hoop earrings and bought way too many pairs of converses.

I will never forget the first time I wore a tie and suspenders; I felt my confidence reach heights that it'd never reached before. I did Shane things, walked up to girls at the club and introduced myself while giving intense eye contact "I'm Khanyisa, but you can call me Khanyi". Confidence works! First faked, then I grew into it. I walked up to straight presenting women, asked for their numbers and they gave them to me. I kissed a lot of women, all women – even the Korean women got some lip action. I was in my element; black, woman and queer. It turned out I was not going through a phase when I used to dress like a boy in high school, that's who I was. The phase was the dresses and high heels; my debilitating need to fit in even when it costs me my authenticity. I finally came out to myself in Korea. I was fully myself, unapologetically me and made a vow to never be anyone else again.

Chapter 4

The Lion City

I met Alex Mcclear in July 2006 in Cape Town, Durbanville. She was in South Africa as one of twenty American college students who came as missionaries with the Impact Movement – that's the Christian movement I was a part of in university. The Americans spent about a month in Cape Town hanging out at orphanages, conducting "summer camps", which I guess would be winter camps for us since they came in June, and played with the kids at juvenile centers. I did not even know we had juvenile centers in South Africa, we never did any of this before the Americans came. Juvenile centers are brutal, sad, and scary. Eight-year-olds in prison for having done some heavy shit! I met a ten-year-old boy who was in there for stabbing another kid, he was reserved, scared, alone and I couldn't for the life of me understand how we, as a society, have no other avenue for these kids than prison! I cried that day, I went back to dorm and cried!

I met the Americans in their second week in the "mother land" as Americans, particularly African Americans refer to Africa, and these students were all African Americans. We were on our winter break when they arrived. We knew we would meet them when the break ended which was something to look forward to when the month in Cala started to feel a bit too long. I was one of the leaders of the Impact movement on my campus, thus making me one of the ten people who would be taken to the guest house in Durbanville to meet the Americans. Alex walked into the room about five minutes later than everyone else, wearing baggy sweatpants, a pink sweater that had a big "S" on it, a black bandana that covered most of her head leaving out a few curly pieces dangling on her forehead and an infectious smile. I went over to say hi and my heart flooded with love. I knew this was it, I had finally felt it: "love at first sight". I wanted to say "Hi, I am Khanyisa, and I love you". I didn't though, I simply said Hi, hoped her heart was dancing to the same beat that mine was, and prayed to Jesus that there was nothing on my teeth!

Our best friendship was instant, it began at that heart throbbing "hello". We spent her last two weeks in South Africa together. I took her to class with me, she broke rules to come and see me, I convinced her it was "cultural" for women to hold hands, she believed me. When the final day came, a group of us went to see them off at the airport, her and I shared a sandwich, that she bought, airport prices are not for students, and we held hands under the table. We hugged, cried, and promised to talk to each other once a week. You will never know how committed you are to someone until you use some of your monthly allowance to make weekly phone calls to America. An email every day and a phone call once a week.

A few months after Alex left, Rato and I started our "situationship". I was so ashamed, and guilt ridden, and felt like I couldn't talk to anyone in my inner Christian circle. I knew what they were going to say, the scriptures they would quote and the judgement that I would endure. I decided to send Alex a confession email.

"Hi, I have something to tell you. I have been kissing a girl. I know it is wrong and I feel terrible. Can you help me?"

Two weeks went by and no reply. I must have written about five follow up emails before giving up. I'd been ghosted. No reason, no email, no phone call, just silence. It took months to finally stop obsessing over my unreturned emails, wondering what I could have said or done for her to just cut me off like that. In 2009, I am sitting at the computer lab on campus, a broke graduate, sharing a twin bed with a girl I am doing lesbian things with but is not my girlfriend. I get a message that says:

"Guess who?"
"Alex Mcclear?" I didn't recognize the yahoo username, but knew it was her.
"Yes, it's me."

It had been a year since I sent those unreturned emails. She was already a not so distant memory; thoughts of her would creep in occasionally. I'd wonder where she is, and why she stopped talking to me. I needed closure.

"Where are you?" I asked.

"I live in Singapore; I've been here for about a year now."

I remembered my neighbor's father, the school principal, yelling at us once for stealing some oranges and he mentioned Singapore.

"You know they chop your hand off in Singapore if you steal. I will send you there if you do this again" he threatened.

I must have been about 10 years old at the time, but never forgot what happens to thieves in Singapore. I then convinced myself that it was a country he made up just to scare us and it worked. Singapore was a very distant memory until this moment; at the computer lab, talking to Alex who was there as a student in a partnership with Stanford and a Singaporean University. It turns out that my neighbor's dad wasn't lying either, well they don't cut off hands, but they do cane for petty crimes. The harsh punishment for criminal activity is what has kept the country as safe and clean as it is.

Alex and I didn't stop talking this time. An email and a text every day, a phone call once a week. This was also during the time I was starting to think about moving to South Korea.

"If you move to South Korea, we can see each other every weekend." Alex said excitedly.

Before making all these plans to see each other every weekend, I had to know why Alex ghosted me, so I asked.

"Why did you stop talking to me?"

"Because you told me about that girl"

"Why would THAT make you stop talking to me?!"

"Because, all my friends, around the same time, were telling me the same thing and I began to wonder if I was also gay. You know that saying, 'birds of a feather flock together'. I was also scared to be influenced by you"

"Influenced by me?! I live on a different continent!"

"I know but before you told me, I noticed that when I talked to you, it didn't feel like I was talking to a friend, I was having other thoughts" Christianese for "I had a crush on you".

56

"Oh, you had a crush on me!'
"I guess you could say that, but I knew it was wrong and so I had to stop talking to you."

That was it, I got my closure and our plans to see each other every weekend resumed. It dawned on us when I got to South Korea that we had not researched how far we really were from each other. It is a six-hour flight to Singapore from Seoul and it's not cheap. It was however much easier and cheaper to spend way too many hours on skype. The internet in both countries is superior to the internet in all other countries I've been to. We could even watch movies together. No, we were not dating. I had a boyfriend, and she was "focusing on God and men" and plus, she made me promise that I wouldn't fall in love with her. It's a crazy promise to make someone but whatever, I made it, I was straight now. Also, what "straight" woman needs another woman to promise that?! A not so straight one, perhaps?!

My first summer vacation was spent in Singapore. Three weeks of paid vacation! My flight to Singapore was six-hours with a long layover in Guangzhou, China. Guangzhou is where I found out you are not allowed to take pictures at immigration. I had bought myself a new camera. My first ever digital camera and I was using it everywhere. I took it out to take a picture while waiting in line and a Chinese security guard came charging at me demanding that I delete the photo. I was so scared I thought I'd shit myself. I shakenly deleted the photo and wondered if they'd let me go through. They let me through and within a few hours I was landing in Singapore. Alex waiting at arrivals wearing all blue, blue jeans, a blue tank top, a blue scarf over her shoulder, blue earrings and that damn smile. My heart beating outside my chest, and I thought "I'm in so much trouble".

The drive from the airport to her house reminded me a lot of Cape Town. It's not that it looked anything like Cape Town but the energy of the two cities are very similar. As taxi drove through the boastful city lights, the music in the background, and me wondering if she can hear my heart beating, Alex said:

"You have a sexy voice."
"Uhm, thank you," I said nervously.

I've never been complimented on my voice before and what did that even mean, my voice makes her think about sex?! After what felt like an hour of my heart beating a little too loud, we arrive at her place, Ang Mo Kio.

"We will share my bed, I have this body pillow to put between us and you'll have your own sheet," she instructed.

"Okay cool."

A body pillow is *actually* a thing that people buy, and I didn't know but it's perfect for single people who like to cuddle. It did do its job of creating the much-needed barrier between Alex and I. That sexual tension she introduced in the taxi when she complimented my voice made its way with us to her bedroom. I always feel restless the first night in a new place, this was no different, but the butterflies made the restlessness a bit more intense than usually. Three weeks of sharing a bed, separated by this long pillow, and pretending that there is no sexual energy between us. I thought I could totally do it. I did after all have a boyfriend at home, Leon and I liked him a lot – I think, although I hardly spoke to Leo during the three weeks in Singapore. She on the other hand, was a straight woman who asked me not to fall in love with her. There was also an Indian boy that she had a huge crush on, Finny. They met in church and Alex wanted to be his wife.

All of this, the boys, the promise, God, guilt, fear, and shame were not enough to drive that sexual attention away. We slept together every night, spent our days gallivanting through the streets of Singapore, went to church on Sundays, visited Alex at work and there it was, unspoken but deeply felt. I also found out that homosexuality is illegal in Singapore. Isn't it fucked up that governments can impose such laws? They can tell you who you can legally love as if that is going to stop us from being gay. This law is obviously not enforced because I had never seen so many lesbians in my life! I joked that they make lesbians in Singapore, that there are factories spread out in the city where they manufacture them.

Perhaps I noticed them because I wanted to be one of them. I wanted to hold hands while we walk around the beautiful botanic gardens, I wanted her to lay her head on my lap while we watched the ducks at the reservoir, and I wanted to big spoon her when we fell asleep at night. Knowing that these are thing I would never get to do; I focused all my attention on enjoying Singapore, which was my first vacation. Singapore is small but there is so much to see and do there. The population is made of Chines, Indians, and Malaysian, but you have to be careful – Singaporean Chinese don't like to be associated with Chinese from mainland China. It's the same in Hong Kong. When you have a complaint, Hongkongese will say "ahh those are people from mainland China, we don't do that here".

Within a week I was able to distinguish between mainland China Chinese and Singaporeans. There is a certain confidence with which Singaporeans present themselves in Singapore, as if they are the only ones that truly belong there and everyone else is their guest. Then there is the rude way that mainland Chinese talk, this is explained by the fact that Mandarin is a rude sounding language. I was offended at first by their impatient demeanor.

"What you want lah?" salesperson asking while you get your food.
"Nothing." I'd reply and frantically look for a nicer stall owner.

Africans are generally known for their warmth and hospitality. I internalize it when service people are being rude to me because I am raised in a society where that is frowned upon. Alex had to explain that they all speak like that and they don't think they are being rude; it's just how they speak. I had to learn to be a little less sensitive, grow a thick skin and decide on what I want to eat fast.

Alex worked for the Singapore government's water agency, she was managing a few of their reservoirs. She was also one of the other three black people I saw that looked like they lived there. She was the only black person in her company because when one of her colleagues saw me, he seemed pretty excited that there were more blacks in his small city.

"So, Alex, she is a nigger from Africa?" he asked with a huge smile on his face.

Did this man just call me a nigger and smiled while doing it?!?

"Yes, she is from Africa, but we don't use that word," she calmly explained.

"Which word" he asks confused.

"Nigger, it's not a nice word."

"Oh, I'm sorry, I didn't know." He apologized, his cheeks giving the Asian glow brought on by embarrassment.

How can a grown man not know that the word Nigger is a derogatory term? I believed him though. He really did not know. I became more curious about what Singaporeans think the word means when an older man, who seemed a little bit more traveled and worldly asked the same thing on a bus.

"So, you girls are niggers," the man asked showing off his perfect English not Singlish.

"Excuse me, what?" I started to frown.

"Well, you are black, so you are niggers. Are you American niggers?" he inquired.

"No, we are not niggers. We are black people." Alex, again calm.

Why did these people think it's okay to use this word so loosely? I realized that the only relationship that they have with the word is through music and movies. It is the same way in which my brothers and their friends used the word. African American artists use it with a casualty that would make anyone outside of the American bubble think it carries no power. It is then confusing for people outside of America to be told not to use that word when they hear it so frequently. At least two Singaporeans now know and hopefully they've told their friends. Maybe no one will be calling me a nigger from Africa the next time I'm in the city. A girl can dream.

As a government worker, Alex was privy to some cool free stuff. One of those were a pass to Sentosa. A beautiful man-made beach with an amusement park. This big people playground is connected to the city by train and it's the best thing for that inner child. Ahh!!! I let little Khanyisa have her time at this place. She went on all the rides, ignored her need to throw up, raced on the cable cars and she ate all the food. A Chinese family, mom, dad and two teenage girls were behind us at the zipline platform. They had managed to convince the obviously frightened mom to zipline with them. Poor woman made it all the way up to the platform only to throw the biggest tantrum I'd ever seen, seriously, she put little people tantrums to shame. It was so bad that the entire family had to turn around and miss out on the adrenaline rush.

It was on the same platform that I realized how popular K-pop is in all of Asia. The cute gay Singaporean man securing my harness lost his shit when I told him I live in Korea. He burst into a K-pop song, as much as I don't care for it, I used to fane interest to impress my students, I was Bonga that he sang the one song that made me seem cool to my kids. It was 2NE1's I can't breathe, and I even knew the moves. This was such a unifying moment, that's what music does. I was a black woman, on a zipline platform in Singapore, dancing to K-pop with a Singaporean, that is the power of music. After our song and dance, the guy had to do his job of making sure I don't turn around like the Chinese woman.

"Okay, are you ready," he asked.
"Yes, no, wait, I don't know," my voice cracking.
"Okay, I'll count to 3..1, 2"

He didn't get to three as he sent me flying, screaming, my legs kicking and heart racing over the beautiful views of Sentosa. Then in seconds, after the adrenal rush really kicked in, I was beating my chest like Tarzan because I felt so good, liberated. Ziplining was on the list of things I swore I would never do. It was one of the things I had labeled "white people things", right up there with bungee jumping and sky diving.

I haven't forgotten about my sexual tension with Alex, I know you want to know what happened. We were walking down Arab street when we bumped into three very tall black American men who stopped us for a chat. I was looking like a tomboy that day, saggy white shorts, a tight t-shirt and flip flops but these dudes still hit on me.

"We must not look like a couple," I teased after we turned them down.
"No, we don't, you're not interested anyway," she replied and clearly not amused.

Wait what?! Does this lady know how torturous it is to sleep next to her every night? We had removed the body pillow at this point but still using separate sheets.
"I am interested, but I have a boyfriend and you're straight." I explained, so confusing. Women can be so confusing! How did we go from, "promise to not fall in love with me" to "but you don't even want me!" How?!

"Okay," she says as her eyes drop to look at my lips.

What is happening?! Does she want me? We had this back and forth for two more weeks until my last night when she started touching me and moving towards my side of the bed. My heart beating so fast, I thought she could hear it, palms sweating, knees week, head spinning, and the butterflies completely out of control.

"I have to pee." I said jumping out of the bed.

I really had to pee. The timing was horrible, but it had to happen. The moment was gone when I returned, all I got was a long, babbling apology. But I left knowing that she wants me!

Chapter 5
Assalamu' ailekum (Peace be unto you)

All I knew about Malaysia was that it was a Muslim country, it was one of those countries I swore never to go to when I was a born-again Christian, or if I went, I would convert all of them to Christianity. I remember ministers talking about false gods in church and one of those gods was Allah, the god of the Muslims. Part of my mission as a devout Christian was to "make disciples" and that meant going around telling people about Christ. When I was in University, part of a campus ministry, converting Muslims was a huge part of our ministry. I knew nothing of the religion, nothing of the people who believed in it but was brainwashed into branding it as bad. Even though I was now unlearning or challenging a lot of what I was taught, I never got to think about my view of Islam until my first trip to Malaysia.

My first trip to this tropical country was a long weekend away with Alex. It was during those three weeks of pretending to have no feelings and that unmovable sexual tension. Alex had planned a fun filled three weeks for my vacation and one of the activities was a four-day trip to Taman Nagara, a rainforest in Malaysia. The eight-hour bus ride from Singapore to Malaysia was comfortable and not cold. Bus drivers in South Africa are air condition obsessed, maybe it's to help them stay awake but you know you have to bring a blanket with you. Our first rest stop was in Johor Bahru, only four hours from Singapore. The bus stopped in front of a building with a restaurant, toilets and a group of men sitting outside smoking and eating.

I got out of the bus wearing a spaghetti shirt and comfortable travel pants, I know you've seen them, everyone who has traveled South East Asia has a pair. Those men looked at me like I was walking around naked. It was like they had never seen arms before. It was only when I walked inside the restaurant and seeing how covered the women were that I realized that in their eyes, I was naked. I wasn't even mad at those men for looking at me. I got it. They had some arm action and a little shoulder show. I however learnt the importance of reading up on the rules of the countries I travel to that day. I want to be informed and I also want to be respectful. I know that I am a guest in someone's home, and as a guest, I need to respect the rules.

After that important lesson on travel etiquette, our bus made its way to Kuala Lumpur where Alex and I booked a room at Dragon Inn. A hotel only a few minutes' walk from the bus station. Alex is a planner! She plans a trip to a t! She thinks of what to do now, while simultaneously deciding on tomorrow. My brain does not work like that, which works for us, she helps me to plan for the future, while I remind her to live in the present. This trip was no difference, the reason our hotel was so close to the bus station, is because we would have to take a bus to Taman Nagara in the morning! As the name suggests, Dragon Inn, this was a Chinese hotel, located in China town.

To my surprise, right there, in the middle of Chinatown, was a Nandos. A South African chicken chain with the best T.V adverts in the country. I wouldn't normally go crazy over a Nando's at home but anything that resembles home when you're traveling sends joy to the soul. Even better was the music. You have to be from South Africa to recognize that the music they were playing at this Nando's, in Malaysia was 'umbhaqanga". Umbhaqanga is Zulu traditional music, a genre I don't usually enjoy at home, but I loved it in Malaysia. You know it's umbhaqanga by the very first guitar cord, each song starts like that, a quiet strumming. I had been away from home for three months at this point and didn't know how much I missed it until I ate that lemon 'n herb chicken. I wasn't even home sick; I was told that it's something I should expect but I hadn't felt it yet. I was only three months in with a whole year to go.

Walking around Chinatown as the only two black people in the area was challenging to say the least. Chinatowns are generally crowded because of all the cheap knock offs you can buy. This was my first Chinatown experience and I decided then and there that it would be the last. There is no walking space, hardly any breathing space and the vendors are extremely aggressive. They all want to scream at you, not talk, scream at you, force you to buy shit you don't need and get mad when you don't buy anything. It's just a lot for me.

"Where are you from?" the vendors would ask.
"South Africa."
'Aaahhhh WAKA WAKA!" they would sing looking at me to join in.

I loved that they knew where South Africa is and I had the 2010 soccer World Cup tournament to thank for that but I couldn't sing along with them because I was sure they knew the song better than me. All I know of that catchy Shakira tune is "waka waka ee" that's it! A lot of them were even selling vuvuzelas. I hate vuvuzelas. I know that's an unpopular feeling to have as a proud South African but goodness those things are loud. And here I was, thousands of kilometers away from home turning down eager vuvuzela sellers. I couldn't feel about the vuvuzela the way I felt about Nando's, they didn't bring me the same sense of joy.

After a long night of looking at fake brands, we went back to our very Chinese hotel to get ready for our bus ride to Taman Negara. I didn't know what a rainforest is but was very intrigued by the idea of floating restaurants. We were up early because I have a reasonable fear of being left by my bus. I've never missed a bus, or a flight and I have my grandmother to be eternally grateful to for that. She would wake me up an hour earlier and rush me like I was late.

"If you don't leave now, you'll be left behind," she'd say in panic.

I can still hear her whenever I have to go somewhere, and that old lady's voice has saved me from having to book another flight because I missed mine. It has also made me ridiculously early for things, there's no need to be an hour early to catch a bus. Thus, we were thirty minutes early, got to choose our own seats and wait for the other people to come. We got to people watch, something that I thoroughly enjoy especially at airports. I love to just sit, and watch people do people things like eat their food. Have you ever noticed how vulnerable the act of eating is? The face contorting as you open your mouth to shove an object in it, the chewing, and then the swallowing. I get why some people have a fear of eating in public! I also think you can tell a lot about someone by how they handle their food.

You can tell how gentle or aggressive they are just in the way they eat. This is a habit I got into when I was in university, my friends and I would watch men eat at KFC drumsticks and say things like "see how he's eating, he's a bad kisser". This is when I was a closeted homosexual feigning interest in men but pointing out everything, I thought was wrong with them - which was everything. I even got some of my friends disgusted by how men eating ice cream on a cone, think about, have you ever seen a man look attractive while holding an ice-cream cone? NO. It just doesn't look good on them.

The bus ride was a quick four hours from Kuala Lumpur to where we would get the boat to Taman Negara, I was nervous about the boat ride. I had never been on a boat before and had a very justifiable fear of it capsizing. It didn't help that the boat was a tiny piece of wood that barely floated. I grew up in a family that fears everything. My family cringes when I tell them some of the things I've done. None of my family has visited me because they're scared of flying. My aunt still has a minor panic attack every time she must get on escalators, not the elevator no, escalators.

We arrived in Taman Negara early evening and I had a difficult time seeing its beauty. The first thing you see when you get off the boat are the floating restaurants made of wood and bamboo. Basically, what we call "amatyotyombe" (shacks) back home. They float on a dirty river that resembles one of those rivers I was forbidden to swim in by my grandmother. Alex on the other hand was loving it, she couldn't believe how beautiful it all was. The floating restaurants that looked like they were about to fall over, the dirty river, the kids swimming in the dirty river; all of it.

It is all perspective, isn't it; we were both looking at the same things and experiencing them differently. Alex was raised in the suburbs of Washington DC by doctors. She was in swimming lessons at the age of three, family vacations were in Puerto Rico and no grandmother scaring her out of her adventurous childhood. Seeing Taman Negara through her eyes helped me see its beauty as well. The floating restaurants are truly a sight to behold. Not only were the restaurants beautiful to look at but the food was delicious to eat.

I discovered there what a "rainforest" is. I wasn't sure why Alex would want to go to a forest that rains all the time, it just sounded miserable to me. It's a bit more than just that though, yes, it's a jungle and yes it rains a lot but there is so much to do. There is the wobbly wooden bridge floating through trees they call the canopy walk. It's an hour hike through the jungle up the mountain to get to the canopy walk, I was the last one up. I wasn't physically or mentally ready for any kind of hiking. The last time I'd hiked a mountain was at nine years old when I went to look for my grandmother's cows. She then decided that it's safer for them to graze around our neighborhood because the town was starting to get dangerous. She was worried that I'd get raped up there all by myself, what she didn't know was that my sexual assaulters were in our house. It was so freeing to do it as an adult, out of choice and the desire to see the view from way up high.

One of the famous activities in Taman Negara is visiting a village with indigenous people. I had very mixed feelings about this experience. Though I loved seeing that part of Malaysia and seeing how the indigenous people live their day to day lives, I was uncomfortable with them being treated like things to see, it felt dehumanizing. The young kids lined up to touch Alex and mine's skin and hair. It appears it was the first time; they were seeing tourists that looked like them. One of the other tourists came to sit with us as we played, and the kids just got up and left as to say "no, we've seen too many of you". I was slightly annoyed by her intrusion, it felt like those kids needed to be around us, to see that there are people that look like them in the world. We were also taught how to use a blow gun by the indigenous people. They had a teddy bear nailed to a pole and the challenge was to shoot it in the heart from a far distance. There was a good number of people waiting their turn when Alex, using her hunting skills she inherited from her Native-American side, took the gun and shot the thing right in the heart thus making everyone slowly disappear.

Alex desperately wanted me to swim with her in the dirty river, an offer I vehemently declined. I was among the 80% of black people who can't swim, this has since changed as I realized that water is fun, and its intention is not to kill me. However, in Taman Negara, I was afraid to swim because drowning is a thing, and so is my grandmother's ass whooping.

"Come swim with me," Alex said as she floated in the dirty river.
"No, I can't swim, I'm hydrophobic." I said pulling out that big word 'hy-dro-pho-bic'.
"You sat on a small boat comfortably for three hours, you are not hydrophobic." She reasoned.

I started telling her about how my grandmother used to hit me when I'd go swimming in the river. My grandmother was convinced that I would drown. She had stories upon stories of children who had drowned or been washed off by the river. Looking back now, I'm pretty sure that some of those stories were made up just to sway me from going.

"Aha, you are not afraid of the water, you are afraid of your grandmother," a real Oprah aha-moment.

"Oh shit!"

"She's not here, I promise you, no one will hit you. Come swim with me," she insisted.

Who says no to that? So, with my black shorts and white t-shirt, I dove into that dirty river, flopped around like a baby who has just discovered something spectacular and I came up looking like a girl on spring break. I learnt that day that the things we fear don't necessarily have power to hurt us. Our imagined danger can cause us to miss out on the best things in life, like swimming in a river with the girl that you really want to kiss.

Let's fast forward to when I actually moved to Malaysia and lived in Kuala Lumpur. After my one-year contract ended in South Korea, I knew I wasn't ready to go back to South Africa. I had kissed the girl by now and we were trying to be close to each other. She came to visit me two months after those sexually charged three weeks we had in Singapore. I knew that her attempt to make a move and retract would make her ghost me again and so I made her promise to tell me if she's going to stop talking to me instead of disappearing. We kept in touch, our Skype sessions were between two and seven hours every night. Finny, the Indian boy she liked, was deported from Singapore after a girl in church accused him of making sexual advances at her. Leo, the boy I was dating, broke up with me! The long distance was too much for him and so he did what every reasonable human being does, breakup via means of text messaging. I didn't even cry when he dumped, I was relieved. Alex had all my attention, affection, she ruled every corner of mind. She was my first, and last thought of the day.

I had control over the situation when she came to visit me in South Korea. I had home ground advantage. This time, it was me picking her up from the airport, I didn't have a body pillow and refused to have separate sheets, it was winter, and I wanted to snuggle.

"Let's just kiss and see what happens. We both want to," I said making it a light thing.

"Okay fine," she shyly giggled coming in for a kiss.

"Mmhh I felt nothing, I'd imagine a lot of spark doing this with you," she looked perplexed.

"Let's try it again, you never really know the first time," how dare she say no spark!

We kissed again and this time it was longer, slower, butterflies everywhere even on my toes. That was it for me, I knew I'd be kissing her for the rest of my life. The first time we had sex was as awkward as the first kiss. I basically dry humped her with my leg until she came. I didn't know how to please her; she was a new body to learn. The idea that lesbians know how to please all women because it's the same body parts is simply not true. We still have different kinks; different things turn us on and so yes, it's the exact same equipment but functions differently. All I knew was that I needed to press hard on her vagina.

My closeted sex with my Rato was not adventurous, it was stolen, rushed. There was no romance, no "I like that" or "don't do that". I was more of "I'll take what I can get, quickly". We were always scared of getting caught. She also was a selfish lover, pillow princess of a sort. I did most of the giving, she'd rarely reciprocate, she never even went down on me. Hence, my first time with Alex was awkward, even for me. I was shocked when she got off, it was a pleasant surprise.

"I was shocked when I got off, I kept thinking if this was it until I orgasmed," she said.

"Yeah girl, there's more," Khanyi was always trying to appear cool, in control.

It wasn't an easy journey from those moments to deciding to live closer to each other. There was a lot of crying and repenting done by her to God. I had been through what she was going through, I did all the crying, promising never to do it again, thinking I was going to hell, but no amount of praying made me straight. I was at a point where God was going to have to love me gay or not love me at all. Having gone through that made me patient and compassionate with Alex. I was also convinced that she was worth the patience. The back and forth went on for about a year and a half. We were still struggling with her Christianity and being gay when we moved to Malaysia.

I went back to South Africa before starting my life in Malaysia. They were impressed by my worldly experiences and my knowledge of the Korean language. I told stories and shared with them my joys of being overseas, but they were still not privy to the information about my sexuality. I wasn't ready for the rejection I knew I would face. Although I was aching to tell my brother all about the American girl, I was in love with, I wanted him to stay proud of me. I knew that sharing this information with my religious family would destroy their impression of me. I was accustomed to their admiration and wasn't willing to give it up. They were ready for me to come back home and didn't take it too well when I told them I'd be moving to Malaysia. The day before I was supposed to fly to Malaysia my grandmother called me to her room to tell me the horrible news she had heard on the radio about Malaysia.

"Nororo (her nickname for me), did you hear about what happened in this country you're going to?"
"No, what happened?"
"A car fell from the highway and landed inside someone's house!" she exclaimed.
"Okay, that's horrible but I'm still going."
"What if that was your house," fear tactics at play.
"Well it wasn't Kuku and if it was, then it'd be my time to go."
"Yho, you will die in the streets," she said giving up.

There was a time when my grandmother's scary stories would have worked on me but not this time. Not only was I older, but I knew I wasn't going to live in South Africa plus, there was a girl in Singapore waiting for my return. I had spent a good month with her traveling Indonesia and as much as I loved the old lady, it was time for me to jet off on another adventure.

Chapter 6

Same Same But Different

UCSI's English program was focused mostly on students from the Middle East, with a few from different parts of Asia, who wanted to study at a Malaysian university. These students were to spend the first-year learning English before they could enroll in a course of their choosing at the University. If you love movies as much as I do and follow the news, you will know that the portrayal of Middle Eastern men isn't always a good one, in fact it hardly ever. It took me teaching these young adults to realize that these were people, with the same fears and aspirations as everyone else. They were kind, naughty, scared, loving, loud and everything thing normal about being a human. I got to learn about their struggles as the chosen villains of Western societies, their war plagued homes and beautiful but also complicated culture.

My colleague and I once decided to organize a cultural exchange class where each student had to prepare a presentation on something, they wanted people to know about their country. One of my male student from Iran chose to explain why women were covered in his country.

"I want to start by giving an example. If I have two candies, one is wrapped and the other unwrapped and I throw them on the ground; which one would you choose to eat." He said grinning, like he was about to blow minds!

"The wrapped one of course." Everyone yelled out.

"This is why women are covered in my country. It makes them decent and good future wives." Boom!

"Wait what?" I said ready to engage.

"Yes, teacher. The women in my country are good women because we cover them."

Deep breaths, very deep breaths! Wwooosssaaahhhh!

"Okay, thank you for telling us about your country. Next please," my colleague chimed in as she saw the smoke coming from my ears.

Being raised in as highly patriarchal society as the Xhosa culture did nothing to prepare me for this moment. The covering of women in Islam is something I had struggled to understand but I also understood it's a struggle that wasn't mine. I get it because there are things, we do in my culture that I am uncomfortable debating with people who aren't part of my culture. I know that initiation school for boys is harmful but the hairs at the back of my head stood when I saw an article written by a white journalist about "umoluko" (initiation). This is a practice where boys who turn eighteen are circumcised and then spent three weeks on a mountain with the premise that they will come back as men. There are boys who had botched circumcision – where instead of cutting the foreskin, the whole penis mistakenly gets cut. We have had boys who get infected with HIV because "ingcibi" (the man who cuts) used the same knife on different boys. Some have died up on the mountain from harsh weather conditions and dehydration.

I was always perplexed seeing tourists from the Middle East though, where women wear Burkas, waiting in the sidelines while their husbands were walking around, swimming and enjoying themselves at the beach. There was an imbalance that I could only explain with "fuck the patriarchy" but to hear this nineteen-year old boy passionately talk about women as candy worried and infuriated me. I was also in a difficult position as his teacher to respect his opinion and what he regards as his culture but also express my confusion. I must have been easy to read because after class he called me to the side.

"Teacher, I know it was wrong to say women are candy and I am sorry. I just wanted to explain why women were covered in my country and use an example," he said.
"Thank you."

In the same breath of having to encounter men who have been entrenched in the bullshit of patriarchy, KL was also full of Nigerian men. This is not an exaggeration, many Nigerian men, and a few Nigerian women, have made KL their home, thus making it a nightmare to be black in Kuala Lumpur. I should insert a quick disclaimer here. I know that not all Nigerian men do the sneaky shit that they are known for, but wow, a lot in KL do. I rented a room at a new condominium building for the first few months in Cheras while looking for a place of my own.

The owner was a beautiful woman named Nadine and our other roommate was Suhalia. The idea that Muslims and Christians (I identified as a Christian at the time) cannot live together is pure nonsense. If anything, we are all so much better for it when we live together in our differences. Both these women were practicing Muslims who prayed five times a day, wore hijabs, Suhalia was a virgin and Nadine was battling the guilt of having had sex before marriage. That sounds very familiar, doesn't it Christians? I will never forget finding Nadine crying during one of her Saturday afternoon prayers.

"What's wrong, girl," I asked.
"I don't think Allah will forgive me for what I did with my British ex-boyfriend," she said unable to control her tears.
"What did you do?"
"I had sex with him, and I knew it was wrong."
"Doesn't Allah forgive us even before we ask for His forgiveness. It might be that you are struggling to forgive yourself."

How often do we do that? Project our feelings about ourselves to the God. I did this too when I was Christian. Let my shame overshadow everything I believed God to be because I was unable to forgive myself. I'd talk about a good, kind, loving, forgiving God and then in my personal life, live as if those qualities were not extended to me. This is what Nadine was doing with her spiritual life.

Both Nadine and Suhalia were the ones to knock on my door on Sunday mornings to wake me up for church. Suhalia slept with her light on because she was scared of ghosts. Nadine couldn't convince her to turn it off and settled for buying her a side lamp. We became close Suhalia and I, her family lived far from the city and she'd visit once a month. We spent most of our weekends getting lost in Kuala Lumpur because even though she had a GPS in her car, we didn't know how to follow it. It got to a point where we'd buy snacks to prepare for the hours, we'd be spending in the car getting lost. We celebrated like teenagers when she broke her "hand-ginity"; the first time she let a boy hold her hand. I loved that sense of innocence this 27-year-old approached love and dating. Her grandmother would send her back with durian cake to give to her "African roommate" every time she went to visit. Nadine on the other hand had to keep me a secret to her family.

"Khanyi, I'm sorry but I have to tell you this. My father would be very angry if he found out that I have a black person in my home. They don't visit me often but when they do, it's better if you're not here." She confessed looking ashamed.

"Sure, I'll be your secret," I said jokingly easing her nerves.

I had no problem being Nadine's secret, it was kinda thrilling. Plus, I now had two women keeping me a secret. Alex who I was being gay with and now Nadine, who I was being black with. Like most condominiums in KL, this one had a good number of Nigerians. I made friends with these guys because they were nice and had good internet, but the internet was the main selling point. All these guys did was swimming in the rooftop swimming pool and work out at the gym.

"What are you doing here?" Prince asked during one of my nightly visits where I brought my computer to chat to Alex.

"I teach English." I replied slightly perplexed because I was sure I'd told him what I do.

"No, I mean why are you living far from home. You are a good-looking woman; you should be home, and a man should be taking care of you."

"Don't ever say that shit to me again." I said angrily packing up my computer.

"Okay fine. Do you want me to tell you how to make more money?"

"That's better. Sure, tell me what you do."

"I scam people on the internet."

"How?"

"There are a lot of ways to do it but I use Facebook mostly, flirt with girls and get them to send me money."

"Why is that okay for you to do? You're such a Christian, all your posts on Facebook are about God. Do you think He's okay with you scamming people?"

"Yes, He knows I need to start somewhere to provide my family the life they want when I go back home."

"Thank you for telling me Prince, but I will not be involved in that. This will also be the last time I'll be coming to your house."

"You're being stupid. You don't even know how much money you can make simply because you hold a South African passport."

"That's okay. Let me be dumb and feel good about myself."

The actions of men like Prince made finding an apartment of my own exceedingly difficult. Most ads clearly stated, "we don't accept Africans." I am in no way saying that the Malaysians were justified in their ignorance, but I could get where it was coming from. I tried to trick a homeowner once by saying I was Alex from America. The conversation went well until towards the end when he said:

"Sorry I have to ask. Are you African American or white American?"

Shit! I knew where he was going with this and I couldn't exactly lie since I'd have to meet him to view the place.

"African American."

"Oh I'm sorry, we don't rent to Africans."

How was that even legal?! However, Legal or not, it was happening. There was no place in Malaysia that didn't treat me as another black person and place whatever stereotypes they had about black people on me. I had western union agents refuse to help me because "they don't send money to Africa" who only did because the American, Alex, threatened to sue them for discrimination. Church friends who didn't know if it's okay to call me black as to not offend me but would rather call me "African" WTF! Countless moments of having to teach and challenge.

"I am black so you're not offending me. We have white people in Africa and they're also Africans. Africa is a continent not a country that's why I sound different from the other African 'brothers and sisters' in the church. No, not all Nigerians are bad people who want to steal your money. Yes, the N-word is very offensive," and so on. I felt very black there, like, my blackness was the first thing I was judged on in all my encounters. Even from the nice people who thought it was such a cool thing for them to have "a black friend". Like, the defining virtue of our friendship was the fact that I am a black person.

After a few weeks of being rejected, I finally found an apartment. A beautiful three-bedroom penthouse in an old run-down resort complex. The outside walls of this five-story building looked like they hadn't been painted for years. The peach color it previously was, was seeping through the peeling green. The inside of the penthouse made up for the outside. It was an open concept kitchen and living room, with two bedrooms and even had a wet kitchen. All it needed was a paint job, new couches, new bed frames and a whole lot of love. I wasn't happy with the steepness of the hill to get to my new home but told myself it'd be a good leg workout.

Time was ticking, Alex was coming back to Malaysia and this time, she wasn't going back to Singapore. She had quit her job and was moving in with me. We agreed to decorate one of the rooms in a way that made it look like someone lived in it. That's the work you put in when you're in the closet. Her fear was that my colleagues would know we're a couple if it was obvious that we lived in the same room. Forget that the colleagues I'd eventually want to invite to my home were an openly gay man, a bisexual woman, a very open-minded British woman and a man whose sexuality we all questioned. Her fear of us being "caught" overshadowed the facts of who our friends were. We did all the home fixings we wanted, painted the rooms, decorated the living room and when it was all done, invited our new friend group to our new-ish home.

"Who sleeps in that room," asked Amy, the open-minded British woman.
"I do." Alex replied.

"Oh, I see." Amy struggling to hide her surprise.

As the night progressed and the amounts of alcohol being consumed increased, Amy had the courage to say.

"You guys, we know you are a couple, and no one sleeps in that room. Why are you pretending?"

"Well, it's scary to be openly gay in this country so we figured it was better to just say we're friends." I lied.

"You don't have to hide from us though, it doesn't matter," she said downing what I think was her fifth glass of vodka.

I can't put into words the feeling of relief you get from not having to lie to the people close to you. I knew they had their suspicions, but it was freeing to finally say "yes this is who we are to each other" and to have that proclamation met with love and acceptance. My gay friend Hamza was also happy to not be the only homosexual in the group. He had spent most of his life in the closet, only out to a few other gay Muslims. It is more than just hard to be a gay person in Malaysia, let alone being a gay Muslim. Hamza told us about the time his father was angry at him for using tissue to wipe the sweat off his forehead. He, the father, thought using a tissue was feminizing and wanted his son to use his forearm like a real man.

This is the level of discomfort this man had about his son's femininity. I still wonder if Hamza will go through his plan of marrying a lesbian Muslim just to get his family off his back about having a wife and children. His plan seemed plausible and made sense. Choosing between family approval and being authentic is not so easy for some of us. This is what made me come out at twenty-seven years old. It was not an easy coming out, my family is very religious and very homophobic. I did it because Alex and I had been together for almost three years and it didn't feel good hiding the person I loved from them. I was so in love and wanted the people close to me to know who I was that. I wanted them to share in my happiness. I was not okay hiding who she was anymore and loving her made me master up the courage to come out.

"Ncinci, I have something to tell you. Alex isn't just my friend, she's my girlfriend. I'm a lesbian." I sent her a WhatsApp text.

"You are going to hell, that's not natural," she replied sending my heart to a weird space of pain and relief.

I was in pain for what she said to me, the long text that followed was horrific and ended with "don't tell your grandmother about this, it'll kill her". Her and I are close, she basically took over raising me when my mother died. Reading her response to my coming out broke my heart. However, I was relieved that I had finally said it. Coming out for me, felt like I had released something from my chest, a load that I didn't even know I was carrying. I felt light, I felt free and above all, I felt like I had given myself permission to be myself. As much as my aunt's hate haunted me for days, I was in a loving space that helped me heal. Love does cover a multitude of sin.

I can only imagine the challenge that awaits Hamza should he decide to come out. He was still too young to have to have to think about that yet. He had new friends: black and lesbian. Our house became his haven, and he could be as gay as he wanted to be. Malaysia slowly became home, and I had a close group of friends who became my family. These are people from different backgrounds and what I will always treasure, is that our differences didn't matter. We were okay being a family of different races, cultures, religions and sexualities. It was so fascinating to me that we were in one of the most Muslim countries in the world and this is where I learnt what it means to truly accept people for who they are. I really had to unlearn everything that I was taught about Muslims in my Christian upbringing. I can honestly say it is all bullshit and I feel bad for people who continue to hold uneducated and ill-informed views about Muslims.

However, even though this was home, the money I made was not enough to make me overlook the fact that I was slowly getting worn down by the Nigerian men who asked Alex and I to marry them every day. I know this sounds so petty but living in an apartment complex with them as a majority became overwhelming. There was not a day where I wasn't turning down a marriage proposal or I wasn't being followed down the hill when I went to work in the morning. One guy hit on me at 7am with his eyes covered in eye boogers. It wouldn't have been so horrible if our safety wasn't being threatened. It felt like it would just a matter of time before someone knew where we lived and began to bother us at home. So, after a great nine months in this tropical city, we made our way to the next destination.

Chapter 7

Pura Vida

After a thirty-two-hour flight from Kuala Lumpur to San Jose, with a five-hour layover in expensive Amsterdam, the first person to greet me in Costa Rica was a homeless brown skin woman who excitedly yelled "NEGRITA". Well she was the third. The first two were Alex and our friend Minaj. They arrived in Costa Rica a day before me, since they flew in from The United States. I landed in at 8pm, with a suitcase, a backpack and loads of excitement. I couldn't wait for the morning to come so I could explore San Jose, Costa Rica's capital city. I woke up in the morning with a bounce in my step, my dreads flowing like strings of glory and a smile that refused to go away. As I walked, I mean glided through the streets in the morning for some Costa Rican breakfast, arros con pollo (rice and beans) my third greeter emerged; "NEGRITA".

I didn't need to speak Spanish to know that this brown lady was calling me a negro. The irony was too big to ignore. I kept on walking because I wasn't going to let this woman ruin my child like excitement of being in Central America. There has never been a sexier language than Spanish, but not Spain Spanish – that collective lisp is not sexy, Latin American Spanish, that's sexy. You can tell that Latinos know that their Spanish is sexy. The way they speak in movies, their swag even when sad or angry. The ways they curl their lips when they say something as simple as "aaii papi!" – sexy!

My first reaction to being called "Negrita" was offence. The word, in English, is filled with so much hate and has a very painful history for black people. However, when I took a look at this woman, she was smiling as she called me "Negrita". As if she was happy to see me. I later learnt that the Ticos (Costa Ricans) used it as a term of endearment. My Spanish teacher, Roxanna, explained that Costa Ricans loved being brown skinned and that's why their statues of Jesus and Mary were brown. They wanted to worship dieties that looked like them. Her and her husband lovingly called each other "Negrita" and "Negro" which just mean black!

Alex, Minaj and I came to Costa Rica to study at the University for Peace (UPeace). This is a UN mandated university beautifully built on a mountain in Ciudad Colon, a town only forty-five minutes outside of San Jose. The UN chose Costa Rica for the university because it is the only country in the world that doesn't have a military thus making it "a peaceful country". This is a notion that my classmates and I would fiercely challenge because even though there is no military in Costa Rica, their police are heavily armed. Every corner in San Jose is patrolled by policemen and women who carry big ass guns with ammunition making the whole notion of a "peaceful country" null and void. The fact that a few of my school mates were robbed in Costa Rica and some at gunpoint didn't help in enforcing the ideal of a peaceful nation.

A group of us used to love going to the lesbian clubs in San Jose, majority of these women were straight by the way. We would get off the bus and start running from the bus terminal to town central because the bus terminal is where most of the criminal activity took place. These are things that I never worried about in Asia but because they had armies, the UN didn't brand them as "peaceful nations". The only bad thing that happened to me in Malaysia was a guy trying to grab my laptop bag while he was on his motorbike; cowardly but effective. It didn't work on me though; I had my hand tightly gripped on the bag. Safety was not guaranteed in Costa Rica and the school administrators made sure to tell us that on the first day of school as well. Imagine how confusing it was to be told that we had to be careful in this crime ridden, peaceful country, what a paradox.

Costa Rica was full of contradictions; one of them being that the country is thought to have the happiest people. I do not know how that is decided and who does the voting but from what I saw, there was nothing "happy" about Costa Rica. One must understand the intersectionality between poverty and criminal activity to understand that Costa Rica should not have been on that list. I still don't know what deems a country "happy" but I felt that that was a strong statement to make for a country like Costa Rica.

I heard locals complain about the economy and how the influx of Americans retiring in Costa Rica has made everything expensive. I do know that title of "the happiest people" does not incongruent with Costa Rica's socio-economic plight. There is an undeniable sense of fear that hangs in the air as one navigates the streets of San Jose causing a real feeling of unhappiness. I don't know about you, but I am not happy when I'm scared. Ciudad Colon had ongoing campaigns on suicide prevention, big banners on the main road with a toll-free number. When I asked Roxanna about this she simply said.

"We are not a happy country. If we were, then why would we have this campaign? People are not happy here."

I was also taken aback by the not so subtle racial discrimination that Ticos had towards people from Nicaragua and the Caribbean coast. A group of us were excited to go to a carnival that was taking place in Limon. Limon is a small town in the Caribbean coast next to Puerto Viejo. We were all discouraged by the people we were staying with in Colon because and I quote "that is where all the black people are". This was a major mind fuck for me because Ticos aren't white either, some of them are darker than me. One of my friends was told by his host family, "Don't go there, those monkeys are criminals."

This reaction made it more intriguing for us to go. We were a bunch of students at a school that encouraged us to challenge popular opinions like that, so we had to go see these "monkeys". We were not surprised when we got there, and the town was full of black people. My people! And when I say black people, I mean really black, like *black black*, like Africa black. The town felt black, the energy is vibrant, the accent sexy Spanish meets Patwa and the sound that comes out is heavenly. Limon is what listening to Reggae music feels like, you just want to walk around with a coconut infused with rum and dance in the street – my friends and I did just that. Our weekend was fucken amazing. Carnival was exactly what I had imagined it to be. It is a straight gay pride parade. The entire Caribbean coast showed up with colors, feathers, food, music, and we were there for all of it.

The only "criminal" activity that happened was someone snatching my friend's camera at the parade and that could have happened anywhere. I don't know why the people of Limon have such a bad rep in Costa Rica, no I do, it's because they're black. Maybe or even definitely, there is crime in Limon, but it doesn't make it more or less crime stricken than other parts of Costa Rica. I feel like there is not a place you can go to in the world where black people are not confronted with the burden of their skin color. We are black before we are human, we are always having to prove ourselves, prove that we are not criminals, prove that we are not loud, prove that we are not angry, prove that we are deserving. It is exhausting.

Our university was its little haven though, to a point where it would feel like we weren't even in Costa Rica. The student body was made up of a hundred and fifty students from forty-seven different countries. The first day of school felt like an international airport, each of us trying to figure out where to go, different accents and languages in the same space. There were the suit and tie types who obviously went there under the illusion that they would work for the UN one day and the hippies who honestly believed that they would learn about how to obtain peace. I was sort of floating in the middle with no expectation. That has always been my emo, the ability to shift, to maneuver, just so I can fit in, a chameleon one might say.This shape shifting power might have helped with the damage I did to myself when I was a closeted lesbian, the tenacity with which I tried to fit in the Christian space was soul crushing.

All the courses were centered around the topic of peace – I studied Gender and Peace Building. I am a skeptic when it comes to world peace, and the university didn't do much to change that skepticism. I went to the University as a product of my environments and the environments of the people I'd met along the way. How could I even think about peace when I'm from a country where people are killed over cars and cellphones, when I held my student from Syria whose best friend was burnt for defying the government? My nonexistent hopes for a peaceful world were further crushed when one of the professors said "a peaceful world is a utopia". I was shy to speak in front of all these people who seemed so smart and well versed but when he said that I had to raise my hand.

"A Utopia you say? Can you give a dictionary explanation of the word?" I asked.
He started to giggle knowing where I was going with the question and explained, "it's an imagined place where everything is perfect; something that can never be obtained."
"Then why are we here." I asked and an applause ensued.

From that moment, I talked myself into thinking that I was there for the experience; it truly was. How often does one get all those different cultures, countries, backgrounds, mindsets, values and everything that makes us human, in one place?! The University for Peace did it and we lived in peace, mostly.

Chapter 8

Half of wisdom is learning what to unlearn.

My course ended up being one of the best decisions of my life. I got to label a lot of the things I'd been feeling but had no vocabulary for; we are more aware when we can name a thing. I can now explain to anyone what heterosexual privilege is and how it affects me as a gay person. We discussed everything under the sun; race, religion, sexuality, compassion; all of it. There are days where class went over the allotted time because the discussions were heated. Some of the classes would end with my best friend and I mentally turning tables. Like that one time a student from Nepal said Nepalese people get HIV from the Indians or the time Swedish who said woman who stay in abusive relationships are just lazy.

I learnt about the cast system in India, sexual dysfunctions in Japan, skin bleaching in Jamaica and South Africa. One of my favorite professors, gave me the best way to define myself and I will forever be grateful. She called herself a "failure of socialization". She explained it as "not being what you know you were raised/socialized to be". That resonated with me and I own it. Women in my culture are raised to look forward to getting married, make sure they don't have a child before marriage so that their bride price doesn't get lessoned. You know this from a very young age, as soon as your breasts start to show - you hear things like "zavel'iimpondo zenkomo" (the cow's horns are showing). Bride price was traditionally paid with cows but with modernization, it is now cold hard cash. I also knew that being married would mean adhering to social gendered norms (also learnt that term at UPeace) and I would fail at those as well. Thus, in the words of Professor Sharat, I am a failure of socialization.

I had naively thought that we would all have similar views and share the same opinions about life. You can then imagine my shock when during the first day of orientation, Joshua from Cameroon randomly yells out during his group presentation, "I believe that marriage is between one man and one woman." I am sitting in the front row next to my lesbian lover, at this school that is supposed to be super down with that and here is this young Cameroonian man bravely voicing out his homophobia. I heard my jaw hit the ground with disbelief, the disbelief turned to disappoint, and that turned to rage. I was angry that Joshua perpetuated the stereotype of a homophobic Africa, disappointed that he crushed my anticipation of being in a gay loving space. This is not how this school was supposed to roll y'all! These people were supposed to be open minded and accepting.

One day I am sitting at the school cafeteria having lunch with two of my professors when Sister Miriam, a catholic nun from Kenya comes at me with the same bullshit.

"I think God created marriage to be with a man and a woman so that they procreate." She starts.

"What about couples who can't have children," I ask.

"Well then they can just enjoy companionship."

"But that's not the purpose of marriage, it's to have children, you just said that." I argued.

"God shows them mercy by letting those couples enjoy companionship."

"But He is angry at homosexual couples who enjoy companionship because they 'can't have kids', it doesn't make sense to me."

This conversation went on and on with two of the professors coming to my rescue. We talked about the different genders that exist in the world and of course Sister Miriam thought that was a bunch of crap. The only thing that got her to like me after that day was when she realized who I was dating. She really liked Alex and that was enough for her to tolerate our "lifestyle". What I still value about UPeace was how much people evolved in their thinking as the year went by. I don't know if Sister Miriam has changed her views on homosexual love, but she became one of my favorite people at that school. She came to house parties with a bottle of red wine, told stories about life at the convent and even attended the vagina monologues.

It was also Sister Miriam who gave me the first hug when I gave a talk on being gay and Christian. I had always been conflicted with the idea of a loving God that will send me to hell because I was gay. When I decided to stop praying my gay away because it wasn't going anywhere, I pulled back from the church. At this talk, I told my story of growing up in a Christian household, the shame I felt all my life until I removed myself from Christian circles. In preparing for the talk, I had to be careful not to offend anyone, the gays or the Christians, so my story was about me and my personal journey. I don't think the Christians were pleased with how I talked about the apostle Paul.

I explained that although I loved Paul's writing on love, I disagreed with his writing on human behavior. Paul endorses slavery, has some twisted views on women and is obviously a homophobe. I also tried to find something that Jesus said about homosexuality and found absolutely nothing. My talk was thirty minutes of me feeling brave and vulnerable. I don't think I changed anyone's mind about religion, neither the atheists nor the Christians but we were able to sit in one room and hear each other out. It is the power of conversation that had Sister Miriam and I hugging while we both knew that we disagree on some things.

It wasn't just the people who held different views from that I butt heads. I was once in a heated argument with my Indian friend Raj who hit on Alex while I was sitting right next to him. Raj is proud of how he was raised by a very progressive mother. His mother is a strong LGBTQI ally in their community, and she raised him to be the same.

"Alex, you're very hot. I'd hit on you if you were straight." said Raj, ignoring the fact that Alex's girlfriend was sitting right there.

"Raj, I find that very disrespectful, you wouldn't say that to anyone sitting with their boyfriend." I said feeling the rage inside pick.

"Yes, I would and come on we're friends, why do you look angry?" he says smiling.

"I find your compliment disrespectful; I think you could tell her she's beautiful without overlooking the fact that I'm sitting here." I said.

"Well, Herald and Kate are sitting, and if I felt the same way about Kate, I'd say that." Raj trying to prove his point.

"No, you wouldn't man, and you know it," said Herald puffing up his shoulders almost daring him to.

"I'm very sorry Khanyi, I didn't think that would offend you," said Raj after arguing.

I had been in situations where men hit on Alex before and it didn't work me up as much as this instant did. I would even prepare for it sometimes, especially when we would go clubbing. Alex, who is not a big drinker would take the drinks her admirers buy her and give them to me. She would finally tell them we were together when they would not leave her alone or I would chime in when I was done drinking. A few of them would get mad, understandably so, it was not a nice thing to do. It was fun to watch them sulk as they walk away though. Raj was different, he had been around us for a few months, had spent nights in our home and was someone I considered a friend. I didn't expect a friend to be hitting on my girlfriend even if he thought it was funny. I needed him to know that his advances were disrespectful and careless. I hope he did get it.

My sexual liberation came into full effect in Costa Rica. I was open about my sexuality and loved how sensual I was but didn't know how much work I still needed to do in that area. Sexual liberation is about knowing that your body is yours and yours alone. It is about owning your sex, owning your kinks, and feeling no shame for being a sexual woman. For so long, the message has been that sex is for procreation, this was the message I got from church. It was to make babies or please your husband. Being someone who doesn't date men, my sex is completely different from that narrative, I had thought about sex differently

When I came out, I heard about a phenomenon called "the lesbian death bed", this is where a long-term lesbian couple stops having sex and lives like best friend. I convinced myself that women crave emotional support, whereas men tend to be more physically driven. Alex and I have had our dry spells, but our emotional connection was always enough to sustain them. There is a study that showed that gay couples have more sex, followed by heterosexual couples and then at the bottom, lesbian couples. I have definitely experienced the lesbian death bed. You know you are not having sex when you have to remind your partner when the last time you had sex was.

If you don't know, the vagina monologues are a play written by Eve Ensler. It explores consensual and nonconsensual sexual experiences, body image, genital mutilation, direct and indirect encounters with reproduction, sex work, and several other topics through the eyes of women with various ages, races, sexualities, and other differences. The first time I heard about the vagina monologues was in South Africa through a T.V interview with one of the women who were part of the cast that was in the play. I remember my discomfort every time she said "vagina" but also curious about what the vaginas had to say. When I joined the production at UPeace, it was nothing like I had expected.

I was sitting in a room with women who had different stories about their sex and who shared those experiences openly. Our Wednesdays were spent sitting in a circle of sisterhood, sharing, and doing activities centered around sex and sexuality. We openly talked about what turns us on, what we are attracted to, our sexualities, our sexual traumas; it was a revolution. It got to a point where some of the men on campus were intrigued and complained about not being invited to our circle.

"Isn't feminism about equality? Why are we being excluded?" they would say.

We practiced the actual monologues on Friday afternoon; I was the angry vagina. It started with "my vagina is angry, it's pissed off…." I would get into character, say all these things about this angry vagina and feel empowered. Some of my friends wrote their own monologues! They went into some vulnerable places and thought about what their vaginas would say. On the night of the show, we courageously, with the help of some good tequila and juice, talked about our vaginas. One by one, on the stage with almost one hundred people watching, talked about our vaginas. It truly was a sexual liberation. I am forever grateful for those women. I openly talk about sex now; I talk about it from a place of entitlement to pleasure. There is no shame attached to my sex and sexuality.

I learnt a lot of things about life in that year at UPeace. I learnt that to coexisting with humans is not dependent on denying difference rather the opposite, coexisting is creating space for difference. I always think of puzzles with this, I think how they wouldn't be fun if the pieces were all the same. That's what co-existence is to me, pieces of a beautiful puzzle in the world creating a perfect picture. We can live in this world with kindness and compassion while we hold different truths and opinions.

There were a lot of heated debates in and outside of class but what kept us going back was the understanding that we are all from different backgrounds and a lot of views are informed by those backgrounds. I also learnt that we need to be willing to unlearn a lot of shit to be accepting of others. Our perspectives are shaped by our experiences from childhood to wherever we are now and being fully accepting calls us to unlearn a lot. When I was a born-again Christian, I was taught to not associate with people who are not because "we should not be equally yoked with unbelievers".

I have since let go of those beliefs and my UPeace experience only elevated my need to fully co-exist. It was my Muslim friend Aisha from Morocco who told me about the feminist movement within Islam and I wouldn't have even considered such a thing had I been trying to avoid "the other". I also learnt that people cannot and should not be judged based on the places they are from. When my friend Dawn from Nigeria invited Alex and I to her home, I was sure she was going to give us a bible lesson on why we were wrong.

Nigerians are known for being homophobic, "correctional rape" is still legal over there, so we, Minaj and another friend tagged along to dinner - we needed backup. When we got to Dawn's apartment, she had spent the whole day making us some amazing food and was totally okay that we brought uninvited guests. She just wanted us to be in her home, eating her food, talking about why she loved us and was not a homophobe even though she was a devoted Christian. I felt silly thinking about the time I spent thinking about how I was going to respond to her homophobia, that week was agonizing. The girl just wanted to chill and feed us!

I also learnt that sometimes people are willing to change beliefs they grew up with when they see they stem from prejudice. My friend Jordan from Lebanon came to school upset one Monday morning and she broke down crying telling me she confronted a priest who was preaching hate towards gay people at her church.

"I am so upset that I grew up thinking like that, Khanyi. I wasted so much time hating people I didn't know until now. I remember how it was you and Alex who were my very first friends when I arrived here. You were literally the first people to talk to me on that bus and I was so nervous but felt okay after meeting you and how you were smiling at me. So, when the priest was saying those ugly things about gay people at church, I raised my hand and asked if he had ever met gay people? He said no and I said well I have and that's not how they are. We argued and I left."

People can only learn from and about you when you are being you. Jordan was confronted with her religious beliefs and the truth of who I was, and she chose to believe me because I was authentic. This was my year in Costa Rica, a beautiful mess where I learnt that we are all just people and we should treat each other as such.

Chapter 9

Two suitcases and two backpacks

What do you do after you graduate with no money in your pocket, and student loans to pay? You backpack through central America, couch surf the whole damn thing and put whatever you need to on your credit card. At least that's what Alex and I did. There was no way we were going to miss out on taking two months to travel through central America. We packed up our room in Costa Rica, which by the way, I know is also in Central America, but it was its own experience. We shipped what we needed shipped to America, and we were each left with a suitcase and a backpack. There was no reason for us to have so much shit leaving Costa Rica, did we really need two non-stick pans and all those knives?!

Alex's grandparents' attic has no more room for any more boxes. I love shopping but I like to give my things away whereas, she is a hoarder, big time. There are things in those boxes that would have been better thrown away or given to people who needed them. I know better than to argue with someone who still has their stuffed animals from when they were a child. This could also or mainly be because of how we grew up as well. Most of my clothes were hand me downs from my older cousins and the same clothes would be passed down to my younger cousins so the idea of things being mine forever is foreign to me. I am used to passing things on with the hopes of getting more. Whereas Alex, growing up as the only girl in a monied household, got to keep her belongings and store them. We had boxes sent to America from Singapore, South Korea, Malaysia and Costa Rica.

I am an easy-going traveler, mostly because I hate planning and that means I go along with whatever has been planned. All I had to do for this trip was write to people on couchsurfing.com and decide who was safe to stay with. Remember, a traveling lesbian couple is just two women traveling alone. You can be a group of ten women as a matter of fact and still be "alone" if there is no man around. We have to look for accommodations that are not only gay friendly but where we think we would be physically safe.

Anyway, that was my job, Alex was to plan the rest and I just do whatever she needed my help with. She is a type-A personality, perfectionist is an understatement for this chick. Everything was planned to the T. We even knew which countries were notorious for being violent and planned to avoid them. El Salvador was not going to be graced with our presence. What I didn't anticipate was that we would experience racism in some of the countries we would visit, until our landlord, Runulfo said we would.

"You girls know that they are racist in these countries you'll be going to?" Runulfo asked obviously aware that we didn't know.
"Racist, towards whom?" confusion sweeping through my face.
"Towards, you know, black people," he stuttered because calling me black might be offensive.
"Uhhmmm, they're not white either, they're the same complexion as us."
"Well, they are racist so just be careful."

Runulfo's warning was not enough to make us change our plans. We were going to bus our way through central America, racism or no racism. Plus, I struggled to understand how brown people's prejudice towards other brown people could be. I have found through my travels though that it is more than just possible, it is a fact and an absolute mind fuck. I can mentally dissect being discriminated against by white people, colonization has helped me with that rationalization but brown people treating me differently because of my skin color is confusing and infuriating.

Racism is at the fabric of South Africa; we are to this day experiencing the remanence of the apartheid era. I did not experience apartheid to the extent with which older black South Africans have but I did have incidents that were racially charged. There was a time I was peeing at a mall in Cape Town, I walked out of my stall and the white women waiting to pee didn't go in the stall I was using. It was a minute occurrence but enough for me to notice it. I wasn't the least bit surprised, I washed my hands and watched them almost pee themselves because they were racist af. Having to deal with being treated in a discriminatory manner by brown people has an opposite effect in my psyche though, it drives me up the wall.

Our first bus took us to Nicaragua! There is a saying in Xhosa that goes something like "int'wemnandi'yaphindwa" which loosely translates to, "if something's good, you repeat it".

This is what Nicaragua was for us—a good thing. We had come to this sexy country with two of our friends during one of the school breaks in Costa Rica and spent a long weekend at Lake Apoyo. Oh yeah it is a sexy country! Walking down the streets of Granada makes you feel sexy. The colorful colonial buildings and the small brick roads give the town character and make you feel like you're somewhere in Europe being pretentious as fuck. We may have gone a little overboard with the whole repeating thing business because we stayed at the exact same hostel, we had stayed at the first time.

Hostel Paradiso is perfectly located on top of a hill giving you an unobstructed view of Lake Apoyo. The food at the hostel's restaurant is surprisingly delicious and you have full access to the kitchen if you're a budget traveler like we were. This time we spent a whole week there, just waking up and watching the sunrise, kayaking around the lake and praying we don't capsize. We capsized the first time we went, and it was really scary. We were Bonga to have two muscular Australians behind us ready to rescue the damsels in distress. I am a very functional swimmer; in that I will only swim if I know I will touch the ground should I decide to stand. Capsizing from a kayak in the middle of a lake is not for functional swimmers.

You have to hold your breath long enough for you to push the kayak off of your head and then get back on it! I was against kayaking after that, I didn't like the feeling of almost drowning, I also didn't like being pulled out by strong men. I'm that lesbian who will struggle to open a bottle cap than ask a dude for help. I'm no one's damsel and to make sure I would never be again, I said "no more kayaking". Alex loves to kayak, and it was either she gets someone else to do it with her or I get over my fear and do it. I chose the latter because pride will have you killing yourself. We didn't capsize, thank the ancestors and she didn't do any fun tricks that would cause us to like jumping out to take a dip. We just sat on that kayak, let the sun have its way on with our beautiful black skins and build some biceps while we're at it.

The hostel was also great for meeting fellow travelers. Every night was spent at the hostel's restaurant talking to strangers about where they've been and what they've done. If we were not talking with random strangers, we were playing the games provided by the hostel because really, there is only so much you can do for a whole week on a lake without getting bored. This was one of the many times we were asked for a three-some, at this peaceful lake. It was one of those sociable nights, strangers talking like they were old friends. I drunkenly let it slip that we were a couple and one of the male Spanish travelers interjected.

"Oh, you guys are a couple?" I could feel his excitement as his eyes lit up with curiosity.
"Yep."
"Are you open to a three-some?" he asked seriously.
"No, we are not." I said.

I get incredibly annoyed every time I am asked for a three-some by a man. I am open to three-somes, with women but not one woman has ever asked. I am bothered by dudes offering because it makes me feel that they don't respect my relationship. I feel like a lot of times, men don't take lesbian relationships seriously and they feel like it's for their entertainment. I have had men who openly proclaim that they are homophobes but with the same breath, will talk about how much they love lesbians.

The only way I could explain that is that most men think that we exist to fulfill their sexual fantasies, or that the absence of a penis somehow invalidates our relationships. This is a problem when our sexuality is thought of only in terms of how we fuck as if that's the only thing that makes us homosexuals. I used to get all up and arms every time a three-some offer was made to us but that changed. I know that I am fighting a losing battle with that; now I just breathe and remove myself from or simply say "no".

As much as I love Hostel Paradiso, I did have one complaint. The walls are too thin, not ideal for loud sex. We were in one of their private rooms, but it didn't feel private. We heard everything that was happening in the reception area from our room and I was sure that people would hear us if we had sex. There are moments of involuntarily going back in the closet when you're traveling, and this was one of them. In trying to make sure that we didn't get hurt or experiencing any form of homophobia, we hid the fact that we were a couple and said we were just friends. There are forms of homophobia that aren't violent in nature; the uncomfortable stares when we hold hands, or even the comments about how pretty we are to be lesbians. I can't tell you how many times I've been told that it's such a waste that I'm a lesbian because I'm so pretty.

One man once said, "but you have such nice hips", I realized later that night that he was saying that I have baby bearing hips and therefore can't be a lesbian. There are women who announce that they have a boyfriend once they find out I'm a lesbian, because me being a lesbian automatically means I want them. Staying at hostels like this one, with the thin walls means no sex for a few days or quiet sex, I hate quiet sex. Honestly, now that I think about it, no one would have cared that we were lesbians at this hostel. We were mostly afraid that they might and instead of being bold and showing up as ourselves, we leaned into the fear, shrank, and hid. I'm done with that shit! Okay, back to Central America, after a week in Lake Apoyo, it was time to pack up again and head to Belize.

Chapter 10

My people are your people.

The overnight bus from Nicaragua to Belize had a few stopovers at those "dangerous" countries. We sat on the bus while our passports were collected by immigration officers at the different borders to stamp them as we drove through. We did have a four hour stop in El Salvador to change buses and get some food. I replayed the stories I heard about El Salvador from friends who've lived there, and I decided the furthest we'd go is to the McDonalds that was only 100m away from the bus stop. Getting off the bus we were greeted by a small brown older El Salvadorian lady who said:

"Wow, beautiful but black," this was in Spanish, so Alex had to deal.
"Thank you but you mean 'beautiful and black" shade!

The lady didn't get that Alex was being sarcastic and she kept smiling, looking back at us as she made her way to wherever she was going. It was probably a place where there were no black people, or the black people were not considered "beautiful". I don't want to say that this lady was racist, I don't know her, but I did think her comment was racially motivated. She was shocked that people can be black and beautiful, we were an anomaly for her. Her comment made me curious about how black people in El Salvador were treated. Was Runulfo right about the racism in these countries? That it matters what shade of brown you are in central America. I knew it to be true for Costa Rica, remember the "monkeys" in Limon but I didn't dare think this rang true for every other country in Central America.

When we arrived at the immigration office in Belize, Alex and her American passport make it through no questions asked. I had read that I don't need a visa for this country, so, why was the immigration officer making me wait and looking at me like I had done something wrong? Oh man, immigration officers make me feel worse than police officers sometimes. They look at you, look at your passport, look at you again, flip through your passport, flare their nostrils, look at you one more time, then they either stamp your passport or take it to some office. Why do they have to be so intense?!

The pretty immigration officer with that yellow bone glow did this to me but instead to stamping she went to an office leaving me sweating, imagining everything I could have possibly done to be denied entry in freaken Belize. She came back and asked me to go to the office to talk to the big boss. People say I look like my dad, I don't see it most of the time but I know I smile just like him and that smile has gotten me out of so much trouble and I used it here. I walked in that man's office with the biggest smile on my face.

"Hi!" I said like I was seeing an old friend.
"Oh hi, you're from South Africa," he asks while dividing his attention between me and the soccer game he's watching on the T.V.
"Yes, I am."
"Oh, I loved watching the World Cup. Your people look just like my people. You know we all come from there right, all of us here in Belize, we are originally Africans,".
"Yes, I do, I'm so happy to be here."
"Let me stamp your passport, welcome home sister!" he said extending his hand for a shake.

I shook his hand, struggling to hide the confusion. I thought I was in trouble, that maybe immigration laws changed overnight, and I was going to be the first person they were implemented on. But no, this man just wanted to see an African from Africa with an African passport, shake her hand and welcome her to his beautiful Belize.

Our first stop in Belize was a small farm in Blackman Eddie, I love the name of this small town, Blackman Eddie. Eddie must have been a badass blackman to have a town named after him. At least that's what I told myself, Eddie was a G! Our bus ride from Belize city to Blackman Eddie was a good hour. It was a packed bus with people standing and some leaning over our faces as we were Bonga enough to get seats. As the bus rolled in, I saw a small church with a sign that read "HOMOSEXUALITY IS A SIN" painted in red.

I felt the thing in the pit of my stomach, the thing you feel when you're scared of the unknown. I took that sign and inscribed it on every Belizean on the bus, every Belizean became a homophobe to me in that moment. I forgot all about our friend Coelete who was not homophobic and was from Belize. I read that and thought, well, they must ALL think the same. This is why we introduced ourselves as best friends when we met our couch surfing host, Linna, and requested she prepare two beds for us.

Linna was a single older lady in her early fifties and she owned a big farm. Her farmhouse was everything I had visualized when I thought of a what a farmhouse should look like. The kitchen was something out of a dream, rustic and modern with pots and pans hanging from the ceiling. Linna is a beautiful, black, Belizean woman who speaks English with a British accent and has two of the most beautiful dogs I had ever seen. Her farm is a massive piece of land. She has to use her quad bike or a horse to get around. The words "hard working boss ass bitch" are written across her forehead.

Linna was more than ready to receive us. She drove her truck down the mountain to pick us up and the smile on her face was welcoming. Dinner was already prepared by the time we got there, and she had a genuine joy when she gave us a tour of her home. Her hospitality reminded me of what my grandfather taught me about welcoming strangers. Whenever someone came in to ask for water, my grandfather would insist on giving them food as well. He said "you must be kind all the time, you might be entertaining angels".

I believed Linna when she said, "my home is now yours too". You know how people say that and within three days you feel like you've made yourself a little too comfortable. Not Linna no, she invited her favorite niece Denice to show us around and do the "fun" things she felt she was too old to do with us. Denice was as pleasant if not more. Her perfectly straight white teeth brightened up the room when she said "hello". She was off from school for two weeks and was more than happy to be our "tour guide". Denice made us promise that we would not go to Belize city without her because it's dangerous for tourists.

"Denice, we look like we are from here, no one will think we're tourists." I explained.

"Oh yeah they will know. You are black but trust, you don't look like you're from here!"

She was right. We took the bus to Belize city to buy hair extensions for Alex and I felt like a tourist. I don't know how people knew we were tourists regardless of how much we looked like them. It's possibly the same way that man in Ethiopia knew I was South African without me even uttering a word. I think each country has its own vibe and the people can tell when you're not vibing. Denice was there though, taking us to some local spots and making sure we were eating the best local food. Ahhh the food in Belize!

I didn't think anything would be better than Linna's breakfast, fried jacks. Fried jacks are a Belizean breakfast dish, it's deep-fried dough served with cheese and bacon. I was making those babies myself by the third morning with Linna's supervision of course. But there we were in Belize city eating and eating and eating, feeling like I was gaining weight with every meal and not giving a flying fuck because Belizean women are rocking them curves like African queens. Those women were fully and proudly curvaceous.

There is something comforting about being around curvy black women who wear their curves so gloriously. It's like, the curves are the best part of their bodies and they want to show them off. I am not someone who has intense body image issues, but I would be lying if I say I have none. Being in Belize made whatever weight issues I had seem insignificant. Belizeans wore their blackness with the same pride as well. It's in the way they walk, talk and act. The streets were booming with all things black from shea butter to hair extensions to the women sitting on the streets doing each other's hair. It felt like I was strolling down the streets of Johannesburg, feeling like I belonged but knowing that I didn't.

Linna and I would spend morning sipping on coffee and talking about her life - her amazingly colorful life.

"You know people call me 'the lesbian that lives on the mountain' here," she said, and I knew where she was going with this.

"Oh really, I giggled. It's the cargo shorts and horseback riding," we both laughed.

"I know that you two are not just best friends by the way and I don't know why you are trying to hide it." I shivered expecting the worst.

"What makes you say that?"

"It's obvious, you can't hide attraction, no matter how hard you try to," she laughed.

Linna was so wonderful about knowing we were a couple. She was so sad that we felt the need to hide and spoke about her gay friends.

"I don't get people who are homophobic, it's none of their business," she said frowning.

That conversation ended with Linna inviting herself to our wedding in Bali because she was sure we would get married.

Linna had taken such a liking to us that when we told her we'd be going to Placencia for a week and a half she said

"No, you don't need all that time there, just go for 4 days and come back home," she insisted, and we didn't fight her.

We just packed one backpack to Placencia, leaving the rest of our things at the farm, at home. Placencia is a beautiful coastal town located gorgeously on the Caribbean coast. You know what that means?! more black folks! We were still on our couch surfing budget, but would you believe me if I told you that in Placencia we couch surfed on a yacht!? Yeah, we absolutely did.

Eric was an older Norwegian who had sailed his yacht from Norway all the way to Placencia and decided that he loved the place and stayed. I had some reservations about Eric, an older white man in a town full of brown women. He fit the stereotype of an old white man who goes to third world countries to have sex with young brown women. That image gets pounded in my head every time I am in South East Asia. I saw scores of young Asian women and young gay boys being used for sex tourism.

I thought that's who Eric would be, and I was so off. We booked his yacht because, well it's a yacht and I figured he wouldn't try anything with two women. He also had a glowing review from a group of five European girls on couchsurfing.com and that somewhat put some of my discomfort at ease. Eric was like a fifty's gentleman! Isn't it sad that we have to go back to the *FIFTY'S* to reference how a gentleman should behave?! But that was Eric. He came to the bus stop, grabbed the big backpack I was carrying, took us to dinner, paid for it and then loaded us on a dinghy to take us to his yacht.

This was a three-bedroom yacht with a kitchen, a shower and a dining area. This village girl was at a loss for words. I couldn't understand how things were working out, I still don't really. The first night was rough, yachts are appealing until you have to sleep and realize how unnatural it is to be sleeping on a floating device. As expected, we woke with the worst imbalanced feeling, our equilibrium all shot, and were ready to find a hotel.

"Eric, thank you so much for hosting us but we think we will get a hotel. We aren't feeling good and we're nauseous," Alex explained.

"Oh, I'm sorry but you don't have to go. I have these patches you put behind your ears and they will help you with that. How about you give it one more try?" he pleaded.

"Okay, we'll give it one more try."

We put those patches behind our ears and boy did life on the yacht become better. We were okay inside and outside to the point where it didn't even feel like we were floating anymore. As my grandmother would say: Izinto zabelungu!! (White people's things!!!). We were real yacht girls, bikinis all day, beer on the deck watching the sunset, morning swims for Alex and hot coffee for me, it was paradise. Eric had the week all planned for us and he was happy to show us around.

The first two days would be spent in Palencia and the last two we would spend at his private island – an actual private island! Every time we would walk around town, I would feel the need to defend him especially from the other tourists. I could see them looking at us and insinuating that we were young local girls being taken advantage of by this old man. The locals knew who he was, and we were introduced with pride to all his local friends. He knew the places with the best friend jacks for breakfast and the best crab for dinner.

We sailed the yacht from Palencia to Eric's private island and I did most of the driving. The yacht has autopilot, so I didn't have to do anything, but I felt so powerful "driving" it. Sailing the big ocean on a private yacht with my girl in her bikini fucken surreal, like what is life?! Eric filled the quiet moments with tales from sailing with friends and his solo conquests of the ocean. It was a beautiful six hours of sailing and chasing the sunset. Eric asked us to not bring anything to the island as he had prepared everything already.

He co-owns the island with his friend, and they were building two identical villas. The plan was to bring their families there but make money as well by renting it to the rich and famous. The place was a grown person's playground with jet skis and snorkeling gears. He taught Alex how to create her own waves and then jump over them with the jet ski. Me, oh you want to know what I was doing? I was not driving a jet ski at its top speed in a circle to create waves so I can jump over them, no, I was watching. I enjoyed cruising on the thing, with my life vest on – easy does it baby.

"Babe, I just saw a shark!" Alex says after an evening snorkel with Eric.

Oh man did she really just say she swam with a shark! I watched jaws and I wasn't about to reenact that movie.

"Are you okay?"

"No, it was very scary. I thought it'd catch me, we locked eyes," she said panting from the swim.

"That's all the snorkeling we will be doing for the rest of our time here," this was not a request.

Can you imagine having to call your partner's family to let them know that she'd been eaten by a shark?! I've heard some sad stories about people who lose their significant other during freak accidents while traveling. I read about a gay couple who got caught in a rip tide while honeymooning in Greece. I can't even imagine the pain of the surviving partner. There was no more snorkeling on Eric's island, but we did drive the shit out of those jet skis.

My time with Eric taught me to trust men in a world that makes it so hard to. On our very last day, he took us out for lunch and while we were eating, a group of tourists started gossiping about us. They were so bad at gossiping, looking, pointing, and giggling. Alex, Miss avoid conflict at all cost, went up to these strangers and started yelling.

"I know what you are thinking but just know he's not what you think he is," she says frowning.

"Excuse me," the woman acts confused.

"I see you talking about us, we are his friends, and it is rude of you to stare and point at us."

107

"Oh, okay, sorry," she says turning her back to look at her friends.

This man made zero advances, there was not one moment where we felt uncomfortable or picked up on him having ulterior motives not even one dirty joke. I navigate the world now thinking that there are many Eric's out there. Men who are okay with buying you dinner and not make you feel like you must thank them with sex. As you can see, the theme of this trip is that we were closeted lesbian, we continued with the lie even when we were with Eric. Maybe he knows now from my Facebook, I'm pretty gay on Facebook, but Eric didn't see the fact that we were single women as an invitation to stick his penis in our vaginas. We went back to Blackman Eddie and gushed about Eric to Linna so much so that we even wanted them to be a couple. We connected them with each other on social media, they met but decided to be good friends. We spent two more days in Blackman Eddie taking in all the love Linna had for before we bussed it to Guatemala.

Chapter 11

Bienvenida a Guatemala

Guatemala is one of the largest countries in Central America and is extremely poverty stricken. The bus from Belize dropped us off in Guatemala City and we had to take the local bus to Antigua. It was impossible not to notice how almost every man on the bus was drunk. It was such a strange thing to witness. It was about eight o'clock at night and it wasn't strange that people drink with their dinner. What got me is the number of men who were drunk on this public bus. This was also very telling me about the state of the country.

South Africa has a problem with alcoholism especially amongst men and especially poor men. It is as if alcohol is their way of coping, dealing with the problem of not having enough – their way of numbing. I remembered how all my uncles, all but one, were alcoholics. The one who wasn't an alcoholic, had his own vices; his toxic marriage and a string of kids that couldn't be hidden from his barren wife. It wasn't just my family dealing with these types of men. The type of men who think the bottle is the answer to everything especially their sense of inadequacy. Being on this bus with these drunk men was both sad and negatively nostalgic.

Not only were these men drunk but were also very short. They were extraordinarily short like they all had a birth defect. I felt like a giant on a bus full of short, drunk Guatemalan men. I spent the whole drive exchanging weird smiles with these men, who wouldn't stop gawking. Men who gawk are so creepy. You know them right; you look directly at them to show them that you can see them watch you, but they keep looking anyway. They make me feel so uncomfortable. The forty-five-kilometer bus ride with us packed in like sardines felt longer mostly because of the men, their alcohol smell and lingering eyes.

We arrived in Antigua around 9p.m. and the guy we were couch surfing with came to pick us up from where the bus drops off. He was a tall, skinny, handsome British man named Mike. Oh, stop it, I know what you're thinking, but Khanyisa you're a lesbian, how do you know if a man is good looking or not. I get this all the time. I can see when a man is good looking, I'm not blind. Plus, when I say a man is handsome, it means he really is, he is truly attractive, objectively handsome.

Mike drove us to his two-bedroom bachelor house. His dark brown furniture, his monotonous all grey kitchen and of course, the play-station. This was a well-kept bachelor pad, everything clean and you could tell it wasn't clean because we were coming, this man loved to keep his home clean. He had bottles of homemade salsa, which he made with his man hands in his man kitchen. Mike felt like those men who were both manly and metrosexual and had no problem with showing just how metro he was.

His clean house, white sheets in the guest bedroom, his well-groomed hair and nice clothes. It was so refreshing to see a man who did not define his masculinity by looking like a dirty piece of shit with no home training. Mike was out there, in Guatemala, showing that his mama raised him right or he listened to his mama. We like to say that as if other mothers don't raise their sons "right". Some of these guys forget all that home training and define their manliness by how society tells them to show it. Not Mike though!

Antigua is a beautiful, colorful, colonial town surrounded by beautiful mountains. It boasts with its immaculate design where old abandoned buildings connect to newer ones. Some of the old churches are used as marketplaces. You truly need to appreciate both the modern and the ancient to understand why this town is worth visiting. I was in genuine awe of how these old building stood there and demanded that you give them attention too. They were like old black women who wear their silver hair like the crown that it is, sexy and you can't help but find them gorgeous. These are how the buildings in Antigua are, it's like they refuse to be ignored just because they're old. I loved how the locals found a way to keep them useful. Venders selling everything; food, clothes, shoes, traditional clothes, knives, furniture, literally everything. We spent a few days in Antigua, enjoying the town and Mike's house before we made our way to lake Atitlan.

Same as Linna in Blackman Eddie, Mike was happy to let us leave our huge suitcases at his house as we explored another part of Guatemala. We packed our backpacks and got on the bus to San Juan where we got the boat to our hostel. The boat ride was a quick fifteen minute ride in the pouring rain with an optimistic captain who was rushing to go back and pick up more people. I wasn't scared at all, no, I was fucken terrified. I kept telling myself that this is not how one dies on vacation, drowning in a lake!? But it is how a black girl who is a "functional" swimmer dies, in a lake, in Guatemala, with her grandmother's voice in her heard "yho Nororo, uyazithanda izinto" (Yho Nororo, you like things!). But obviously I didn't die, I lived to tell you about that boat ride. Thank God and the ancestors.

Anyway, our hostel was a cute little situation constructed with bamboo and owned by the nicest British woman you will ever meet. Angela had been living in Guatemala for about three years now. She came two years prior to learn Spanish and fell in love with the place. She came back, built a hostel and offered free English lessons to the locals. We arrived mid-English lesson. The students had printed their favorite Spanish song and were explaining it in English.

I can still see the smiles from her students. They were so happy learning and she was happy teaching. It reminded me of my teaching days in Asia, only my students were younger and not as happy to be learning and on Mondays, I wasn't so happy teaching. Angela runs her place with such kindness, she takes in couch surfers when she's not busy, she does a work/accommodation exchange with tourists who want to live there. Her hostel is environmentally friendly; it is solar powered, has dry toilets and she has her own garden. I was so inspired by her heart and who she was. She was just kind to everything and everyone around her.

Lake Atitlan is this massive lake that has towns inside of it. I don't know how else to explain that. I can't call them islands because it's a lake. Vague I know but that's all I got. You can town hop on the boats and each town has its own vibe. San Juan is the cleaner town and that's where an orthodox Jewish community randomly chose to reside. They felt a little out of place to me. I didn't expect to see tall, bearded men draped in long black robes stroll down the streets of San Juan. They just showed up there and were like "we live here now" and they do. I was curious if they have assimilated into Guatemalan culture the same way that people of other religions are told to assimilate in European societies.

You think of Muslim women in the U.K or Amsterdam being told to take off their hijabs so that they can "assimilate" as if one needs to disown their culture to be part of another. I don't agree with that. Let's coexist! I also doubt the Guatemalans expect that from the Jews, brown people usually don't ask for such. We allow them to settle in our lands to a point where they forget that they are guests and start talking about how they've "discovered" our homes.

The town hopping is pretty much all you can do in lake Atitlan. We did that, all establishments, restaurants are owned by white people, mostly French, no surprise there. The French are like the Chinese really, but they are a bit subtle about it or maybe not. Traveling through central America, I began to expect that most restaurants I eat at will be French owned and most supermarkets will be Chinese owned. It irked me how the Chinese would talk to the locals, it reminded me of the supermarkets in my small town owned by Chinese people who treat us like we all want to rob them. I'm no thief, but their attitude makes me want to rob them. The French seem to put a bit more effort, a lot of them spoke fluent Spanish and their children had local friends.

Lake Atitlan was a stunning piece of paradise but after a few days, it was time to head back to Antigua. This time we decided to skip the boat and take a bus there which was by far the scariest bus ride of my life. Guatemala, like most Central American countries, has revamped some old school buses from the United States. They have made these buses look amazing; I'm talking transformers level amazing. This death trap of a bus we took was no exception. We were packed in like sardines with the locals and their livestock. You know you're in a third world country when you can maintain more than ten seconds eye contact with a chicken because it's sitting right next you.

This bus ride started off nicely with some stunning views of the lake and the towns but turned into something out of a horror movie real fast. The mountain got steeper and steeper. The steeper it got, the less roadside railing there was. All I saw was rolling hills, kilometers of downhill to what would be my imminent death should the driver make one small mistake. Looking up at Alex and seeing the fear in her eyes affirmed my fear. She is one of those few fearless black people whose dream is to build a hand glider so she can feel like she's flying.

I, on the other hand, am one of the majority of black people who are scared of everything, it took me years to not sweat inside a lift thinking about how it might, possibly stop while I'm inside or stepping on to escalators imagining how horrific it would be if my foot got stuck. I looked around the bus and I kid you not when I say that 80% of the local passengers were sleeping, I mean snoring and some drooling. WTF?! This death trap of a ride got even scarier when the driver had to reverse a little bit because the bus was too big to take one of the curves. I took a deep breath, held Alex's hand a little tighter, thought about my family and was ready to go. The guy did his damn thing though because he'd been doing it for years. However, how romantic would it have been had we actually died on that bus, holding hands and feeling like we had been loved and we loved.

We made it back to Antigua safely, spent a few days there and back on the road to Chamuk Champey. I told you Guatemala is huge and there is so much to see. This was another few hours journey only this time, we were in a van with a few Israeli tourists and a driver who refused to turn on the AC despite the scorching tropical heat.

"Driver, it's really hot in here, can you turn on the AC?" an Israeli guy yelled from the back.
"No, you didn't pay enough for me to use it," the smart mouth driver replied.

That was the last of it, we were all uncomfortable but also scared to argue with this driver. He wasn't scary looking at all, I just think it was the confidence in his voice when he replied. It was one of those that felt like he would follow with "try me motherfucker, try me!" and you know not to try anyone that says that. It turned out that we were going to the same hostel the Israelis were going to and it was of course, Israeli owned. I think it's a national pride thing because I've seen the same when it comes to travelers from other countries as well. Koreans will hunt down Korean owned restaurants and hotels, same as the Chinese. I do it too, as if I haven't been eating South African food all my life. It must be because we are creatures of comfort and even when we are away from home, we desperately crave what is familiar.

There was no need to ask if it the hostel was Israeli owned, there is a huge star of David on the wall and the owner is a loud Israeli man. I was moved with how the owner greeted his Israeli guests. It felt like I'd walked into a big family reunion. It seemed like they all knew each other, the big hugs and kisses on the cheek were heartwarming. We didn't get the same reception; I didn't really want one. Hugging and kissing a stranger after that long drive is not something I would have wanted to do anyway. We must have been a welcomed break from his regular guest demographic because even though we were not included in the enthusiastic greeting; the owner spent a lot of his time entertaining us. Well, it was mostly him telling us about his life, from why he chose Guatemala to being married to a Turkish Muslim woman.

"You know there are hotels in some parts of the world that won't let me stay only because I'm Israeli. These are all in Muslim countries. It doesn't matter that my wife is a Muslim."
"Oh, that's sad." I empathized.
"It is and it's all because of the Palestine war. These people don't understand that we are just protecting ourselves," he explained.

He lost me there because as a black South African, I am more than just inclined to side with the Palestinians in this matter. Knowing that Israel funded the apartheid government and supplied them with weapons also solidified my position. One of my best friends at UPeace was Yahya, from Palestine who grew up at a refugee camp and ended up in Canada because of the war. I respectfully asked the Israeli hostel owner to talk about something else as I have a different position and don't think it'd be beneficial for us to have this conversation.

He reluctantly agreed as he needed me to see his point of view and called me intolerant but I didn't want to, so he opted to tell us about how he ended up living in this gorgeous corner of the world. It is not that I am opposed to hearing views that are in conflict with mine, but war is such a heavy topic and disagreeing with someone from said war zone was not good. Also, I felt like listening to him would be intellectually and ideologically cheating on Yahya.

115

Chamuk Champey is extremely stunning and visually surreal. It is levels of crystal blue rivers and green forests. A natural infinity swimming pool so to speak. Not only is it rivers upon rivers beautifully separated by waterfalls but it's rivers that lead up to caves and jungles where you can swim, tube and drink. It is a traveler's dream with a limited number of tourists. Travelers are weird in the sense that we want to go to places that don't have any tourists. We want to feel like the place is untouched, it's as if it makes us special to say shit like "we were the only tourists there".

We were not the only ones, but it sure felt good to not be in a place swamped with white people like Kuta, Indonesia. I think it's because Indonesia is to Australians what Costa Rica is to Americans. Chamuk Champey is where you go if you want to feel like "it's just you" but you know it's not. It is an untouched piece of mother nature where she can gloat without being disturbed. There aren't a lot of hostels even though it's a backpacker spot. We stayed here for about four days, and we were on that river every single day. We were just there on the river, being our black selves and having some serious black girl joy. We would go back to the hostel and eat all the hummus we could get our hands on because that's what lesbians love to eat.

Okay seriously though, I am yet to meet a lesbian who doesn't like hummus and wine. It's like a lesbian in the days of old looked at the can and said, "well these peas have chick in them, let's make these the peas of choice for lesbians". We took ownership and as new lesbians came through, the first thing they need to know is our affinity to chickpeas. If there were a lesbian 101 class, the first lesson would be on our love of hummus, wine and how to eat pussy. That's it, class done!

Most countries in Central America have these beautiful old pyramid style buildings which are known as the Mayan ruins. These 'ruins' are anything but ruined, they are stunning rock formations that were built by the Mayans and are now protected sites. We went to one of these on our way out of Guatemala in a small town called Tikal. I'm not one of those woo-woo, super hippie people who find everything spiritual, but I felt something incredibly profound when I set foot on the grounds at these Mayan ruins. I could feel the history of these ruins before the impassioned tour guide told us about it. There was a peace that came over me and I didn't want to leave.

As per history of every colonized brown people goes, the Mayan ruins are a reminder of the horrific and traumatic history of brown people. It is the white man's idea of what civilization is that left these glorious structures abandoned and then turned into tourist attraction sites. The forced introduction of Christianity in Guatemala caused the Mayans to flee their homes, the few that lived to flee anyway. The ones who didn't flee or die were stripped of their language, culture, beliefs and were given the good old Bible. This is what Desmond Tutu is talking about when he says "they told us to close eyes, fold arms and pray and when we opened them, we had the bible, and they had our land" that quote is true of every colonized nation still to this day.

My fascination with these ruins might have also stemmed from my fascination with the Mayans in general. On Dec 21 of 2012, I received a Facebook message from a friend in South Africa, I was in South Korea at the time. The message read:
"I am happy to see that you are online this morning because apparently the world is supposed to be ending. Seeing that you are in the future (a whole six hours), I'm glad that once again, the word of God (God of the Christians) is still true."
"Hi, have you read what the Mayans said exactly because I did and that's not what they said."
"I don't need to read anything that's not the word of God or that contradicts it. His word is the ONLY truth," she argued.

I tend to have a lot of patience for Christians like my friend because I get that brainwashing, and yes people, it is brainwashing. The idea that we can have a spiritual philosophy that we are forbidden to question, or research is cultish and brain cell numbing. This particular day though, I didn't have the patience for her because if someone says "yo, go read what these people say, it's kinda revolutionary" I would go google that shit all day. Anyway, in my reading about this "end of the world" saga that frustrated the Christians so much, I found that what the Mayans said was that there would be a shift in consciousness, we will begin to see the world in different forms and our perception will change.

They spoke about the advancement of technology and how this revolution will be directly linked to that advancement. For me, as a traveling homosexual, reading that was exciting because I kept feeling like wow, that is so true, the world is changing and I'm here for that change! And so here I was, almost three years after that conversation on this land that was once inhibited by these people who saw our future and I was elated. And dare I say that the world is changing, and it is changing in ways that are both painful and exciting. Change is supposed to make us uncomfortable anyway.

Chapter 12

A little bump and grind

One of the reasons we did this trip was because one of Alex's best friends was getting married in Cancun, Mexico. We had committed to being at that wedding and so we planned everything around that date. I wanted to go spend time in Cancun because I like to have fun, but Alex wanted to spend her birthday on a beach town called Tulum because she likes to have peace and quiet. I honestly had no interest in going to Tulum, something about the name felt boring to me. Tu-lu-m, why?! However, I am a fantastic girlfriend, and I knew it was shitty to convince her to go to Cancun when she really wanted to see Tulum. I lie, I put up a fight, I lost, and we went to Tulum!

We were picked up from the bus station by an overly excited Mexican man with long hair and a typical beach boy vibe. He put us on a local van while he slowly drove behind us on his motorbike. Another ten-minute drive through a jungle where he had to use his motorbike as the road was too small for the van. Two trips with us and our suitcases and we were at his one-bedroom apartment that he shares with guitars, ukuleles, wood shavings and a dog. Our Mexican beach boy/man was a guitar maker, my first guitar maker at that, you don't think about the people who make this stuff, do you? I don't have a poker face, so I looked at him like, yo, dude, how are we going to sleep.

"Okay girls, so you two can share the bed if you don't mind sleeping together and I will sleep on the hammock," big smile.
I am not lying when I say that the said hammock was hanging above the bed. If you and your person can't have a full conversation with your eyes, then you aren't close enough. We had this conversation, just a quick one-minute eye contact where I said, "oh hell no" and she replied, "oh absolutely not". We struggled with telling our excited host that we would not be staying with him after all. A quick location search and I knew what to say.

"Hey, how close is the beach from here?" I knew we were far.
"Oh, we are about five kilometers from the beach, you can just take the local vans, they're really cheap."

"Oh, that's not gonna work for us, it's her birthday this weekend and we really wanted to be on the beach."

"Ahh, yea I completely understand."

Alex had complete access to all her mom's banking details and this birthday weekend was on her. Alex used her mom's credit card and booked us into a beautiful, on the beach resort in Tulum. Side note: sorry and thank you Dr Bee if you ever read this book. Arriving at this hotel I took everything I said about Tulum back. The place is absolute magic. One of my favorite beach towns hands down. Tulum has everything in one small space. We were a mere two-minute walk to the beach and four-minute walk to the bars and restaurants. The best burrito of my life was in Tulum. It was also in Tulum that I realized I was over travelling as a closeted lesbian.

We were at our favorite restaurant, it's our favorite because we never went anywhere else, when I saw these two beautiful women with their beautiful son and the envy, I felt was indescribable. These women were not flaunting their gayness, but they were not hiding it either, they just were. They were two women, at a restaurant, watching a soccer match while their son was running around, you know, normal parent stuff and I wanted it too. Maybe not the attention seeking eight-year-old boy but the just "being", the no hiding, the yes, I just planted a kiss on your cheek and didn't look around to see if anyone saw us because I don't care. Yes, I wanted the not caring.

"I wish we could do that," I said.
"Well, I don't wanna die," she said.
"I don't think they want to die, also notice how no one cares," I said.
"Well we do," she said.
"Yes, because gay recognizes gay," I said winning the argument.

I knew this conversation was not going to go anywhere. Even after three and a half years together, Alex was still up in arms about PDA. She'd only do it if we were drunk or hanging out with other gays, but I guess that's not really PDA.

"I didn't do PDA even when I was dating men," she'd say as if that should make me feel better.

It didn't make me feel better, not even a little bit. I understood where she was coming from, people can be mean to us gays but there were places where I felt no one would give a flying fuck and, in those places, I wanted some PDA. My PDA craving was the last of our problems though, meeting her mom for the first time was our first.

Alex had a good relationship with her mom until she told her we were dating. It was more of a friendship than a mother and daughter relationship and it was beautiful to watch. We had been together for about three years when she decided to come out. She'd always imagined it to be an easy coming out story since her mom is a doctor and has loads of gay patients and let's just say it wasn't that easy. It almost felt like she was blaming me for her child's gayness. You can imagine my nerves at this wedding where I was to meet the good doctor as her daughter's +1. We couch surfed in Cancun while Dr Bee and Justine, Alex's younger brother, stayed at a fancy ass hotel. I mean fancy as fuck. The walk to that hotel room was a little too fast, I wanted that corridor to be a bit longer, buy me more time!

There was no turning back though, I was here about to meet this woman who may or may not think I have AIDS. One of the statements that stuck with me during their argument about being gay was that I am from Africa, and I could have AIDS. Yep, it's airborne in Africa. However, the corridor didn't magically become longer for me, we got to the room, knocked and this beautiful, short, silver haired woman opened the door. Alex looks like her mom, and I thought, well if this is how she's going to look at sixty then she will always be a beauty. They hugged while I waited on the side wondering if I should extend my hand or open my arms. She let go of her daughter, looked up at me with a smile and opened her arms.

We hugged, the hug wasn't too short nor was it too long, it was a "hello stranger who is not a stranger". The hug was sweet, but the post-hug interaction wasn't. When Alex was around, we would talk nicely even laugh but as soon she leaves, the tension would settle in, Dr Bee would talk at me but would not look me in the eye. I am all about eye contact during a conversation; look at me so I can tell if you are being true. I could tell she's the same because of the way she was talking to me felt like a struggle for her, like she was putting in extra effort to not look at me. This was going to be an interesting three days.

The wedding was at an all-inclusive two-hundred-and-fifty-dollar a night hotel, which was too much for the backpacking graduates hence the couch surfing. The day passes, all-inclusive of course were one hundred dollars and I milked every cent. The Thursday was the meet and greet and oh lord did we meet and greet. This was the first time I was meeting Alex's best friends, childhood best friends at that and I was nervous. Girls can be mean; they'd smile then go to the bathroom and talk about how shitty you are. I was so excited to experience an American wedding though, a black American wedding to be exact. I'd watch enough movies to know the fun that was awaiting me and boy did they deliver. The cool thing about this wedding was that everyone knew Alex was bringing her lesbian lover. Her friends were excited to finally meet me and some were intrigued.

"I should make you look cool to your friends by speaking like a real African, I'll speak what we call Xho-nglish, that's English with a Xhosa accent," I joked.
"No please don't, please."
She made herself seem cool by telling them how I speak Xhosa, one of the most difficult languages in the world.
"They have all these clicks, like five right, show them babe, say something." She'd say as they wait for the magic.
"Iqaqa lizikiqikaqika ngomqolo kuqaqa laqhawuka uqhoqho" I'd say explaining it is one of our tongue twisters.
"Woooww…that's so cool," boom, my girl is the cool American with the African girlfriend.

Side note: I was told that if you, as a lesbian or man who goes down on his girlfriend, and you can speak Xhosa, you should just click on the clit (love that alliteration). Apparently, it's magical. I haven't tried this because I never think to do it and when I picture it, it doesn't seem doable. What do I do, take my mouth off and then go QH? Or do I do it before I eat, like a quick hello? I don't know.

We made sure we arrived as early as 11am to get the full day pass experience. It didn't matter how late you arrived at the hotel; you'd still have to pay a hundred dollars for the pass. Her friends were kind enough to let us use their rooms to change. After I got through the hugs, questions, shock about Alex's lesbianism and my blood was at its proper alcohol level, I was my best self and I enjoyed every single minute of that wedding. I had met the bride, Nikki and her mom in Singapore one year and we hit it off very nicely. They were on a mother-daughter vacation and Alex was one of their stops. This is where I learnt black Americans call each other's mom by name! God, it made me so uncomfortable, so excruciatingly uncomfortable.

Every time Alex would call out "Judie", my jaws would grind, like that feeling you get when someone is dragging a chair and it makes that screeching sound. In Xhosa we say "undibalekisela amazinyo" which directly translates to (you are making my teeth run) and it's that thing you do with your teeth when you're uncomfortable or embarrassed "hhhhlllllllll". I was calling her Judie at this point, but reluctantly so. She made me feel like family, her, her husband, her kids and their entire family, they were a lovely bunch of people. They were like those TV black families, the dad is super fun, always smiling, dad and mom genuinely enjoy each other and kids like their parents. Let's get real, you can love your parents but not like them. It's just life.

The meet and greet was fun but it had nothing on the fun I had at the wedding reception. I looked fabulous in my suit pants, white shirt, and black shoes because I will always show up as me. Alex looking gorgeous in her purple cocktail dress and heels, #couplegoals even if I say so myself. The bride was dreamy too, like wow, she was stunning. These two got engaged after having met three months prior at a club, got married in six months thus putting the notion of "when you know, you know" in practice. The ceremony was at the rooftop of the hotel giving us the most beautiful ocean and sunset view. The officiant was the bride's godmother who spoke of spirituality and not religion and my little feminist and anti-religion heart was doing a dance.

The ceremony ended and I was ready to go get jiggy with it at the reception. I am known for being a flirty drunk. This is something Alex had stopped fussing over in our relationship, but this wedding was no place for that. Yours truly over here forgot her audience and got flirty with another girl on the dance floor. I was behind this girl grinding when my eyes landed on Alex's mom who was watching. I saw her look at me and then look at Alex and I knew it was time to stop.

"Not the place babe, did you see my mom see you and look at me?"
"Yes, I did but can I just say that it's good and bad that that happened?" smart mouth.
"How is it good?" frown forming.
"Well, her trying to get your attention when she saw that means she acknowledges that we are a couple and she thinks I am being shady," smiling.
"Good point, but please stop dancing like that with that girl."
"Okay."

Look, I can go on and on about how fantastic that wedding was, but I forgot most of what happened that night which means that that wedding was excellent. The Sunday was "do whatever you want to" day so we went to Isla Mujeres, an island opposite Cancun, again, poor beauty. The island is really small with a Spanish feel to it. It's just restaurants and street vendors. It was a good way to deal with the hangover and talk about what we would do at our next stop, America.

Chapter 13
The home of the brave

"The assumption is that everyone wants to be an American immigrant, therefore, people who want to visit the U.S need to prove that they have strong ties with their home countries." This is what is written on the homepage of the U.S embassy website to explain why you need to bring every single certificate you have ever had and why you need to be interviewed. The first time I was denied, I was interviewed by a white man at the U.S embassy in Malaysia who only asked for my name and where I was from, didn't look at the paperwork I had spent days putting together but just said "no". I was so thrown; this is not what I expected. When someone says "interview" I expect those documents to be looked at, examined, asked some questions but no, not this guy. He just said "no".

"Can you explain to me why not please."
"You just look like you will not want to leave the U.S."
"I have a job here, an apartment, I am an English teacher, what would I do in the U.S?" I argued.
"I don't know but I've been doing this job for over ten years, and I know what people who stay there illegally look like."
"They all look like me?"
"I am done with you Miss, the answer is no, next please."

We stood outside the embassy stairs crying because this meant we would be away from each other for two months. We had plans, dammit. My second attempt was in South Korea, only this time, it was a black woman. I was excited by that. I was so happy when it was her who'd interview me thinking she'd be like "yeah sistah, go to America!" She didn't, she said "no".

My third and what was to be my final attempt was in Costa Rica. All my friends who applied were getting theirs and I thought I should give it a go as well. One of the people who worked at the embassy was a UPeace alumni and that helped with getting the visas. I knew I had to have a believable story about my tie to South Africa so when the guy asked;

"How long will you be in the U.S?"
"I'll stay for three weeks because I need to go back to South Africa. I have an internship with the Desmond Tutu foundation." Name drop!

I knew that they may not know anything about the foundation, but they knew the Archbishop. I may or may not have made it up. Don't judge me, I just wanted to go to America! People have done worse, like way worse, like marry people they didn't love just for that American visa. The name dropping worked! They gave me a year and I wasn't even jealous that some of my friends got five and others ten years. I was so excited to finally go.

However, my excitement turned into horror when I arrived in customs at JFK. That airport is so disorderly, so busy, the security personnel are so angry and international travelers look horrified. I felt my joy turn to fear so fast. The lady I was standing behind was being yelled at for some reason and she was sent to some office. I had watched enough American movies to know that she was in trouble, the immigration officer came back alone motioning to me to come over. My hands started sweating and my knees got weak with every step toward her. I flashed her my smile, but it didn't work, she was not impressed by it.

"Why are you here," she asked looking at my passport.
"For a three-week vacation." my voice shaking
"Do you have an address?" still not looking at me.
"Yes," I said reciting Alex's home address off by heart.
"Okay," stamp, next!

I was so disappointed, I had always imagined the immigration officer saying, "welcome to America" and she didn't. I know I should be happy I was let in so easy but dammit, why did I have to get miss grumpy?! I got over it though, Alex was waiting for me on the other side with a big smile.

"Welcome to America, baby." hugs

The bus ride from JFK to central station is a quick 45-minute ride and I was looking through the window all 45 of those minutes. I was tired but couldn't sleep, I couldn't believe that me, this girl from Cala had made it to the United States of America. When we finally got off the bus on 42nd street, I pulled my huge suitcase, grabbed my backpack, and looked up at those tall buildings.

"Babe, you look like a tourist, stop looking up." Alex teased.
"Oh, but I am a tourist." I kept looking up.

Not one New Yorker bumped into me, as if they also know that tourists look up and they should be on the lookout. I was also texting with my brother in South Africa the whole time, the buses have Wi-Fi over there. I had been to quite a few countries at this point, but this was the first country that my brothers were actually impressed by. When I was in Korea, they would ask how I was doing in China regardless of how many times I explained that I wasn't in China.

"Do the people really fly over there in China," Bonga asked me one time.
"I'm not in China and I'm pretty sure they don't fly in China," I'd try to explain.
"No man sis, it's the same thing," he'd always dismiss me.

America had a different appeal to it though. They were genuinely interested in every move I was making. I think it is because of how influenced they are by American culture particularly black American culture. My brothers are hip hop fanatics, they have memorized most of Eminem's songs and let's not even mention Tupac. This is what sociologists are talking about when they talk about the Americanization of the world. It's how McDonald's is on every corner on every city and in every country or why American pop music was on every radio station. There are boys in my university who sagged their pants, wore durags, spoke in a perfect American accent and they had never even set foot in the land of the brave.

It is also how I could make sense of the fact that when I was in high school, instead of going to play sports after school, I was running home to watch Ricki Lake, Oprah, Days of Our Lives and finished the evening off with The Bold and the Beautiful. Every single day! It was this Americanization of the world that had me explaining to my brother and his friends why Alex wasn't okay with the use of the N word in her presence. They casually call each other that and this time, it was done to impress the black American I had brought home.

"Bhuti, Alex isn't okay with how loosely you guys are using nigger."
"Does it offend her? But this is how they use in their movies and music." this again
"Yes, it's like you going to America and everyone call each other kaffir."
"Oh, that'd be so weird and uncomfortable."
"Yeah, it makes her feel weird and uncomfortable."

I couldn't believe this analogy worked on my stubborn brother, but it did. He went to work the next day and told his friends all about how some black Americans don't like it. They all stopped using it around her but their infatuation with America continued.

"Tell me when you arrive at central station, I want to know if it's just like the movies."
"I'm here bhuti, it's just like the movies!"

"Oh, wow sisi, do their houses really have that thing that looks like wood outside and not bricks?"

"Yes, they do!!"

We booked our train to Bridgeport, Connecticut. Alex's mom lived with her grandparents and younger brother in New London, Connecticut but her mom told her she couldn't bring me there.

"I don't want your girlfriend around Granmi and Granpi, they wouldn't understand." she explained.

"You can just tell them we're friends." Alex argued.

"No, I just don't think it's okay. You guys will have to find somewhere else to stay."

The crazy thing about this conversation is that my aunt told me the same thing when I came out to her. Well, this is after she told me I was going to hell. She made me promise that I would never tell my grandmother. My grandmother has seen and experienced so much in this world; I still can't believe that me coming out would be the thing that kills her. If losing five children didn't make her lose her mind, why would me telling her who I want to be with totally destroy her?

I mean, I get the argument, older people are from a time where homosexuality was an actual mental disorder with assigned treatment, but I think we underestimate our grandparents' ability to love us. I haven't come out to my grandmother, but she has asked me questions that hinted that she knew that Alex wasn't just a friend. It was a different situation in terms of not being welcome to the home. Despite her disapproval of my lifestyle, my aunt opened her heart and home when I brought Alex to South Africa.

I didn't have to choose between not coming home or leaving my partner somewhere while I go see them for a few hours which is what I suggested Alex do but for her it was simple;

"If you cannot have the person I love in your space then you can't have me either."

So, we asked, our friend, Venessa's mom to host us for a short time while we decide what our next move is going to be. Venessa is also a lesbian and she is fortunate to have a mom who accepted her. Melinda will literally kill someone that fucks with her Nessa.

When we asked to stay with her, she simply said, of course you can for as long as you need to. Alex and Nessa met in Singapore and were instant friends. Melinda was very grateful that her Nessa had someone in that foreign country and Alex became her daughter as well. Melinda is a beautiful, Latina woman who has a lot of energy. We got in the car and I felt like I had known her for a very long time.

"You remind me of Eleven," she said.
Eleven is Nessa's shady ex-girlfriend who stayed with Melinda and Venessa for a while. I was slightly offended by this comparison because this chick had brought so much drama to their lives.
"I promise you I'm nothing like her," I said defensively.
"No, I'm sure you're not, it's just that hat and guitar remind me of her," she explained.
"Oh, I can't even play this guitar," uncomfortable giggle.

We arrived at her two-bedroom home which is a perfect size for a single parent and her daughter. Nessa was living in L.A so we had her room to ourselves. I loved that house especially the back yard. It had a small gazebo with a hanging bed, perfect for reading. We were also biking distance from the beach and Melinda had two bikes for us to use. The house is also a few minutes from the 'ghetto'. It was a curious thing for me to see and feel that kind of separation in Bridgeport. It was very clear who lived where in terms of money and race.

The area where Melinda lives is not considered 'ghetto' but two blocks after, there's the ghetto. I could feel the difference in the air. Where we were was quieter and hardly anyone in the streets, where as the other blocks were buzzing. Loud music from cars with windows rolled down, women doing each other's hair outside, kids dancing in front of their houses, it felt like I was somewhere in Soweto.

Alex couldn't have left Connecticut without going to see her grandparents and she refused to go without me.

"I want them to meet you, even if they think you're my friend," she insisted.
"Okay, but we are not sleeping there."

We took the train in the morning and planned to head back in the afternoon. Justine picked us up from the train station. The five-minute drive to the house was quick and I was surprised he didn't ask why we were staying in Bridgeport. Alex's grandparents didn't know we were coming but we were a pleasant surprise. Grandpi was sitting on the balcony reading his newspaper and grandmi was in the kitchen eating.

"Oh….is this Alex" grandpi putting down his newspaper excited to see his grandbaby.
"Yes, grandpi…and this is my friend Khanyi"
"Hello Candy"

Oh no, not Candy. I didn't come all the way to America to have a stripper's name. That's the first thing that came to my mind when I heard that, Candy. After this meeting, with the grandparent's confusion over why their grandchild was not staying at home, we were indirectly told to come stay there. It must have been that confusion that prompted Alex's mom to invite us to stay with the family. She hadn't told her parents why we weren't staying there, and it must have been easier to invite us to stay as "friends" than to tell them why we were not staying with them.

I am weirdly grateful that we were invited to come "home". I got to see how a husband can love his wife to the degree with which grandpi loved grandmi. He woke up every morning to get her breakfast ready, oatmeal and coffee. He then woke her up to come eat and take her meds. He also did her laundry, wash and fold. I know that every marriage has its own troubles but watching these two, I could tell that it was years and years of black love. My grandparents had a different relationship. It was not a love marriage; my grandmother was a stolen bride.

132

My grandfather wasn't even home when she was brought for him. His first wife had died and his brothers thought he needed a new wife and they went and got one for him. It is said that he complained about how short she was when he met her. Although my grandparents got along very well, so well that together, they made ten children! They were not romantic like these two, grandpi being the romantic one actually. I sat on the balcony with grandpi some mornings and hear stories about how he got all three of his girls to school.

"I have a lawyer, a doctor and a principal," he'd proudly say.

Knowing how hard it must have been for a Native American to have such high achieving girls, I understood grandpi's pride. As you can tell, grandpi is impressive as a father just as much as he is as a husband. He had this look in his face, like "yeah, I did that! I did that regardless of what I was told was possible for people like me". He'd tell me about how he worked his way up from being a dishwasher to being a chef, how he was the best salesman at his second job at Sears. What a life and what a man.

Chapter 14

'Merica

Americans in America are not impressed with my accent, not in the way Americans outside of America are. I don't like it. I understand it though, they hear different accents all the time. Something I realized in my subsequent visits there. One of the things I loved about Asia is that I stood out, especially in the small towns. I had become used to being an anomaly. I knew that there would be many people who look like me in America and the only thing that would make me special would be my accent but nope they were not moved. That is, except for a Peruvian woman at a Peruvian restaurant where they sell the best arroz con pollo in New London.

"Oh, what is that accent?" She asked
"South African." finally!
"Oh word, if you are African, how come your English is so good," asks the American man behind me.
"We were colonized by the British." why did I say that?
"Oh yeah, but your English is really good for an African," says the man walking out clearly not understanding what "colonized" means.

I know this is said a lot about Americans, but damn the arrogance in their ignorance is truly alarming. It's not that we make fun of them for not knowing things about other countries, that is fine. It is their confidence in that "unknowing" of shit, that attracts ridicule. This encounter with this dude took me back to a South African braai in South Korea.

In walks a group of American soldiers, with their American confidence that borders very closely on arrogance. The leader of the clan walks up to us, a group of South African women and asks:

"Yo, where y'all from mamas," grabbing onto the front sag of his jeans.
"South Africa," we say sounding like a choir.
"Yeah, now where is that in relation to Kenya and Egypt?" he asks.

"It's in the South," my friend Coco replies a sass that only she can reply with.

"Oh yeah, well I'm from da Bronx, do y'all know where that is?"

"Yes, it's in New York," we say laughing at this guy.

This soldier did what any self-respecting man should do at that point, walk away. I can't imagine anything worse for a man than having a group of women laugh at you, not because you told them a joke, but you were the joke. I once heard that men are afraid that women will laugh at them, and women are afraid that men will kill them. I guess this guy lived out a fear that many men have; he was laughed at by a group of loud, tipsy women.

"I matched with him on Tinder, chomi," said Coco laughing.

"Well, it's safe to say that won't work."

I've had so many run-ins like this with Americans everywhere I had travelled, and I wasn't expecting any less in America. I was expecting to hear shit like, "which country are you from in South Africa", "can you see animals from your back yard", "oh but you don't sound African" and I got all of it. One girl told me that I sound very African which I was perplexed by her need to point that out since she knew I am African.

"I'm sorry to say this Khanyi, but you sound very African"

"Okay, which part of Africa and why are sorry?"

"I have a friend from Nigeria, and you sound like him; no offense."

"I don't sound Nigerian because I'm not from there and the only thing that offends me is you thinking that having an African accent is offensive."

All other accents are sexy but an African one is offensive. What?! Also, some Americans do not think they have an accent because they are American. Again, arrogance, thinking that the whole world is at fault for not sounding like you. That you are somehow superior because you speak English with an American accent. I must point out that some of us enforce this arrogance by faking an American accent to prove that we speak "good English". Private school kids in South Africa all sound like they just got off the plane from New York. They are taught in school that they need to have a twang. Not me, I sound African, and I love sounding African. After I sent the video I was asked to record while applying for the job in South Korea, my agent asked that I do it again and try to sound more American. I said absolutely not because I would then have to have a fake American accent every day for a year.

Alex and I decided to take the Megabus and backpack from the East Coast down to the South. This was my third visit to the States, and we had gone to officiate my best friends' Nina and Darb's wedding. They asked the both of us to officiate and it is one of the top ten highlights of the things I'd done in life. This wedding was different from the Mexico wedding. We arrived a week earlier and got to spend time with the beautiful couple and I'm not just saying that because I love them; you know when a couple is collectively beautiful.

Nina had her wedding planned to a T, she left no stone unturned, and she knew what she wanted. Darbs knew not to fight her, but not in a complacent 'oh, I'm a man I don't plan weddings' vibe but more of a 'whatever my woman wants I'm down'. The wedding was a stunning three-day event, where all the days are somewhat a blur from all the white wine we drank. These two said "I do" at a beautiful country club just outside of Boston surrounded by 100 of their friends and family.

It was my first-time being part of the wedding proceeding and in such close proximity with the bride and I have to tell you - I was fucken scared. I didn't know if we were going to deal with a bridezilla situation, we didn't. Nina was calm until the very last minute when she got nervous looking at all the people taking their seats. Her mom sensed the nerves and she showed up to our changing room with a bottle of champagne and orange juice. We drank up and went out to get those babies married. Be warned, if you are thinking of asking me to officiate at your wedding; I will cry. Standing next to these two as they said their vows was beautiful.

After the wedding, we made our way to Washington DC, Alex's old stomping ground. I was excited to finally see the white house and so were my brothers. They kept asking:

"When are you going to Obama's house?"
"You know it's not his house" I'd mock them
"He lives there, it's his house" they'd retaliate.

I went to Obama's house, it is so white. They must regularly paint it for it to stay that white. It is also a tourist attraction, buses full of Chinese tourists and some students all lined up outside taking pictures. We were all in awe of this house. I don't think there is any other country in the world where the president's residences are such a tourist spot. The whole thing was intense, people pushing to get the best photo and when you look up, two snipers are stationed on the roof ready to shoot. I managed to get a picture of the snipers for my brother and he replied:

"Of course, there are snipers, I'm sure those Americans are trying to kill that African" LOL

I secretly hoped Michelle Obama would walk past us that sunny afternoon but no such luck. She is the epitome of class and grace. I wished she would roll out so I could lay my eyes on her splendor. I used to watch her interviews and speeches, awed by her genius and the care with which she spoke. Also, those arms; I stood there that afternoon thinking "if only I could look at those chiseled arms!" With no Michelle in sight, we continued the day, with my personal tour guide showing me the best spots. Washington DC is truly magical. The museums, all free by the way, were impressive to say the least. I love that DC has no skyscrapers and the only thing is the Washington monument, which Melinda called "the penis that runs America". I'm sure you can see why that is, right?

We stayed with Alex's best friend Naja in the neighborhood where Alex grew up. Naja is one of those people who are genuinely full of life, her voice is loud, her laugh is loud, smile is wide and gives tight hugs. You know when she enters a room because she announces herself. Her presence isn't felt, it is heard. Naja is also very straight, I had to get comfortable with talking about straight people sex. She called herself strictly dickly, she'd never kissed a girl which is like….really straight. It has been proven that over eighty percent of women are not straight. Women are allowed a certain level of sexual fluidity by society, a fluidity that unfairly leaves out men. Women are never embarrassed to say that they have kissed, or had sex with another woman, even if they are straight. I have never seen two straight men drunkenly kiss each other at a club, something that women do quite often. I look forward to a time where men can freely, shamelessly, and confidently explore their sexuality no matter what spectrum they are in their sexuality.

Naja is part of the twenty percent of women that are "strictly dickly". This girl had never gotten drunk and made out with one of her female friends. One of those friends is another childhood friend of Alex's, Kaila. We made dinner one night and invited Kaila over for some food, wine and weed. She refused the weed but indulged on the wine and food. We talked all night about how heterosexuals mate. This was the first time I heard about deep throating; it sounds painful.

"I don't like oral sex, I don't have good gag reflexes and I think my mouth is too small for it," Kaila confessed.

"Oh, I love it, it's not that hard just control your gag reflex," Naja said.

I sat there as this conversation went on feeling so lost. Gag reflexes aren't something that us pussy eating women have to think about. I did almost throw up my first time though. I couldn't get over the lingering smell of pee and thinking that's of the primary use of what I had in my mouth. I also didn't know if I should lick or suck. Rato and I had a lot of finger action until one day, she convinced me to try something new.

"The other girls I've 'played' with used to lick my vagina," she said.

We all know that no one out does a Capricorn so my brain instantly went to "challenge accepted". I slowly made my way down there so slow that she grabbed my head and pushed it down. I was there for a good two minutes before coming up for air. I lost the challenge but hey as they say, practice makes perfect. I now think of myself as a professional pussy eater; a muff master if you will.

Okay back to these straight girls and their sex. I am constantly surprised by how few orgasms straight women have. Men need to do better. You know it's rough when a woman has to finish herself off after sex. I've heard so many stories of women who masturbate after sex because their men can't get them to orgasm; I wonder if it's because women have conditioned themselves to be okay with shitty sex or that most men are so selfish in bed that they don't give a flying fuck if the women are satisfied or not. I don't really know, but straight men need to do better. That, or women need to start speaking up, stop faking orgasms. A friend of mine once said "I don't fake my orgasms, why should I reward someone for work done poorly!?"

Chapter 15

Give me that Southern hospitality and charm

It was back on the Megabus after three weeks of netflixing all day and eating all that good food, smoking good weed, and drinking expensive alcohol from Naja's mom's alcohol cabinet. We made our way to visit our friend Derick, in North Carolina. Derick the kindest, sweetest, warmest, loving, understanding, inclusive, radical black minister you will ever meet. He is a perfect blend of grace and strength. A real teddy bear, tall, big but warm and soft. He picked us up from the bus stop in a blue truck accompanied by his cute two-year-old Mali.

I was always skeptical of going to the "South" because that's where I thought the crazies of America were, the rednecks, bible belters, racists and the homophobes. My fear wasn't completely irrational though, Derick told us how a black person was shot at the park in Concord and we refused to go to the park. It was also the first time where I was so aware of my blackness since being in America because fear informed that awareness. I expected to be treated differently in the South, all I had known from American media is that the South is where the bible belt, racist, nigger word using white people were.

I was surprised to see how many black people live in the South. I was also introduced to what is fondly known as southern charm in North Carolina. As tense as the energy was for me there, the people were so kind. The barber who cut my hair asked if he could bless me with the haircut because it was an honor to cut my hair. What??!! All because I was from Africa. He was an African American and I wasn't flattering him when I said he looked Zulu. He really did. The waitresses all called me honey and strangers were not shy to strike up a conversation.

We met Derick in Costa Rica where he was visiting our friend, Andy and we hit it off. Derick came to visit us in the Philippines earlier that year. He stayed for a week and we almost drowned him. He was going through a rough time with his wife and needed to get away so he came to us. I didn't know this until he arrived. I tried to talk him out of coming until he could stay for more than a week. It's basically three days if you think of the day he lost coming to Asia and the few days he spent recovering from jetlag. He insisted, booked his flight, and came to visit.

My friend was going through so much that he had to book a flight from North Carolina to the Philippines for only one week! I get it, sometimes you just gotta get as far away from your situation as you can. The space you are in can become excruciating and the best thing you can do for yourself is escape. Sometimes being away gives you perspective, a chance to look at your situation from the outside. Derick visited us in our beach town, El Nido in the Philippines and neglected to tell us that he can't swim. He will never live down using me as a floating device when our tiny boat capsized. I was using the dry bag to float, and I heard him screaming. I floated myself over to him to share the dry bag but instead, my good friend grabbed my shoulders and used me to stay afloat. Alex swam over, saving both of us. Aaaah, the things we do to stay alive!!

Derick shared with us that his wife of seven years was seeing another woman after that near-death experience. He disguised the pain and discomfort with a smile.

"Her name is Maurine and Steph, my wife, works at her college. They became remarkably close about six months ago. Maurine started coming over to my house all the time; I picked up that their friendship was not just platonic. I asked her if she was in love with my wife and she said no. They finally told me that they are in love. I am still staying with Steph. I want her to be who she is and if she's into women then I want her to explore that." Silence at the dinner table.

When we visited North Carolina, Steph wasn't there. She was in New York with Maurine. The thing about this visit, is that throughout their marriage, Steph, had expressed that she is scared of flying and refused to do it but here she was now, flying to New York to meet her new lover. Love I guess, it makes us do what we think is impossible, it takes us out of our comfort zones and makes us face our deepest fears. I was enraged by the situation but watching Derick handle it the grace that he did help me relax. He had created space for his wife to be herself while they raise their son.

Maurine had become a part of their family. I could tell that the women were sharing the master bedroom and he had moved to the guest bedroom. I still can't believe how much love this man has for this woman. To love someone like that, to know that you are not in ownership of their sexuality, and should they choose to explore those parts of themselves regardless of the pain they cause is unfathomable. But here was Derick, doing exactly that. He looked pass his own pain and focused on creating a loving environment for his son. He calmly passed the phone to Mali when they asked to video chat him, he did what I had never see done before.

One week with Derick and we were on that Megabus again to visit Jossie in Atlanta. When the bus arrived in Atlanta, I whispered "Atlanta, I am going to love you and you will love me back" and boy did I love it. The city felt like a place I'd want to live in. We met in Costa Rica as well. It was the first day of school and I was so excited to make new friends. She stood behind me at the cafeteria and we started talking. Jossie is like those sexy TV lesbians, tight black jeans, loose fitting shirt, feminine but also masculine, she's that girl you know is gay, but you would understand why men would be attracted to her. She is those lesbians with the intense lesbian eyes. Ladies, you don't know what being looked at feels like until you have a lesbian that likes you look at you. I wish that upon all of you – a gaze from a sexy lesbian. You feel so seen, so wanted and it can make you feel exposed as if all your secrets are being found out. It's also reassuring, a stern "hey, I see you!".

"My partner came with me and spent a few days here, it was great not being alone while waiting for school to start," says Jossie making sure she leaves out the pronoun of this partner.

"When you say partner....girl or guy?" I had to ask y'all.

"Oh my, aren't you straight forward, girl," she says laughing.

That was it, Jossie, Alex, and I formed a beautiful friendship. I think Jossie and I were the lord of the lesbians at school. There were "straight" women who were turned on by Jossie, she is just that sexy and confident. I remember we were dancing and grinding on each other at a house party once.

"Oh, this is weird, it's like I'm grinding on myself, we wouldn't work Khanyi, we're too alike."

"Well, I'd do me, wouldn't you do you?" I said.

"Yeah, I'd do me too," she laughed.

I hadn't seen Jossie since our time at UPeace, but when I called to say we were doing a Megabus trip and will be passing through Atlanta, she made sure we would stop over and spend a week with her. She showed up in her old, black Mercedes looking like she hadn't aged a day since Costa Rica. Jossie was so excited to see us, I can still see her smile.

"I'm going to show you my Atlanta this week," she lovingly says.

If you don't love your city the way Jossie loves Atlanta, then maybe you shouldn't be living there. I knew I'd fall in love with it too hanging around someone who loves it so much. We met Jossie's girlfriend Daniela that day and they're beautiful together. The ten-year age gap is not obvious because Daniela carries herself with a lot of maturity and Jossie's playful nature balances their relationship. Our timing was perfect in terms of accommodation. Her landlord, who is also a lesbian, was going on her annual weekend with a group of friends on a ranch. So lesbian. She was happy to let us have her house if we agreed to dog sit for her. We were more than willing to dog sit, we love dogs and her house is stunning, best bathroom ever! The shower is massive, you can comfortably fit five people in there.

Jossie told us about the Martin Luther King Jr Museum and I of course had to go. I was, am and will forever be fascinated with the man. We mapped out our way and got on the train. My senses were heightened being at the museum. It was easy to draw comparisons between the black South African resistance against the apartheid era and the African American civil movement. I was brought to tears looking at some of the horrific images and broke down when I listened to his last sermon. Nelson Mandela is videoed visiting Martin Luther King Jr's grave and I thought about my history teacher when I was in grade 12, his passion when he compared Martin Luther King Jr to Nelson Mandela.

I felt like I was walking on holy ground when I strolled down Aurbun Avenue. Atlanta did a stellar job preserving that part of its history. I saw families, all races, visiting the area; parents telling their children about Dr. King and his wife. I promised my unborn children that I would bring them there and I would take them to Soweto to visit the Hector Peterson museum. Knowing that every generation will get to hear the beautiful words of this man is comforting; his dream of a world that allows all of us to be treated as equal human beings is something that transcends race, creed, sexuality and nationality.

Atlanta was all kinds of fun but gay people fun. Listen, gay people in Atlanta have all the fun. The drag shows are on another level, the lesbian clubs are not some hole on the wall like the ones I've been to in Asia, no, they are different levels of girl fun. The best thing I did in Atlanta was go on a day cruise, on this lesbian's gorgeous yacht with a group of gays and lesbians. The yacht is a three-story situation that is basically a house when you walk inside, and the third floor is a landing strip. The owner is a helicopter pilot that works in Central Africa for half of the year and makes shit loads of money.

144

It was refreshing to see a lesbian living in wealth like this. I know there are a lot of lesbians who work hard and live comfortably but the impression has always been that gay men make money and lesbians "just get by". I was stoked to be in the presence of this yacht owning type of money lesbo. This was my first time hanging out during the day with so many gay people. I still dream of going to Dinah Shore which is the biggest lesbian party in the world. This was no Dinah Shore but being surrounded by that many queer people sure made it feel like it. We cruised down Lake Lanier, ate a lot of good food, danced the day away, swam and had a good gay day.

Our last Megabus ride was to visit Alex's friend, Luis in New Orleans. Luis was turning 30 that year and we planned the trip to end to New Orleans to attend her birthday party. I was so excited to come to New Orleans for two reasons: 1. I heard the food is amazing and 2. That's where Ellen DeGeneres is from. I love Ellen, she is what I aspire to be in so many ways and she helped me realize that being gay is just something that I happen to be. It doesn't define who I can and can't be, what I can and can't have – that's if I work hard enough of course. Let's face it, the playing field is not equal, heterosexual privilege is a factor, white privilege is a factor and male privilege is definitely a factor. However, watching Ellen and listening to her story, the hardships she went through after coming out, I feel a sense of hope.

I binge watched her show when I was in Korea, we had hours of not teaching, called "desk warming" and that's when I got my Ellen fix. It was important for me to see someone be their authentic selves especially after having just come out to my aunt. I needed confirmation that my sexuality doesn't limit my ability to be fully me and have my dreams realized. In that sense, she affirmed my personhood. I loved and still love how she ends her show: "be kind to one another". I take that statement to heart and I try my absolute best to be kind. Okay, as you can tell, New Orleans had to be on my list of places to go.

The bus station in New Orleans is very colorful with all the artwork on the walls. I had never seen a bus station with so much character, each painting showing the different things that New Orleans in known for, mostly music. Luis showed up in her silver SUV, big car to fit her big personality. I can't be the only one who finds small women in big cars sexy. We had planned our trip to New Orleans around her 30th birthday. We arrived a few days before and were going to leave a few days after. All I remember doing in New Orleans is eating. I ate so much food from the day we arrived - to the day we left. I ate things I would not normally eat, all because they were that good. Our first meal was a po-boy from Domilise's and Luis assured me it was worth the long wait in line. We took our po-boys to the bridge where we watched the sunset over the river, and I felt my body get bigger. It didn't end there, the next stop was to get the best beignet in the city, it's a donut covered in powdered sugar. I wouldn't normally eat that because I don't have a sweet tooth and I try to watch what I eat but not in New Orleans.

Luis' party was all Latino themed because she is from Colombia. I've always prided myself on how well I can bachata until that night. There was no faking it there. It looked like everyone took a class or they were competing. They also don't get tired. Oh, can we also appreciate how stunningly beautiful Latinas are, wow. One of the things that Alex and I fought about is how much of a flirt I am. It's those lesbian eyes I talked about earlier. I had also cheated once and trust me, once is more than enough for the trust to go and never come back. However, with Latino dances, it is damn near impossible to not be sensual. I knew I was asking for trouble when a young dancing machine came to ask me to dance with her. I could have just said "no" but how many chances does one get to sexy bachata with a Latina. Let me live!

"That was some sexy dancing babe, made me jealous." She said looking serious.

"That girl looks 18, the dancing looks sexy because it's supposed to." I said sounding defensive.

"I'm just saying, we know how you turn on the flirt when you're drunk."

"Okay, come bachata with me then."

"No, I don't want to embarrass myself, do you see these people?"

Women know the exact words to use to get you to stop doing whatever you are doing, that one thing you did that one time will always come back to haunt you. 'You know how you get when....' It doesn't matter how big or small, you've proven yourself untrustworthy and that will not stop. You would think forgiveness merit forgetting but it doesn't. It is also difficult to stay true to you when you know that sometimes it makes your person uncomfortable and insecure. In that moment, I did what anyone who wants drunk, sloppy sex after a party does, I sat my ass down and watched the sexy people do their thing.

Chapter 16

Three is a crowd, four is fun

After a few more days in New Orleans, we were done with Mega buses, almost done with America, we flew from New Orleans to New York City for one night with a flight to the Philippines the next day. Our gift to Jossie and Daniela before leaving Atlanta was a trip to a sex store. The new couple hadn't been to one and Atlanta has some big sex toy stores – three stories high. We spoiled ourselves with a small purple dildo that we easily fit in our carry-on suitcase. I put the suitcase through for scanning and it got pulled to the side. Panic immediately ensued as I thought, "crap, someone put drugs in my suitcase, I'm going to prison." They take out the big lotion but don't stop looking.

"Hey, something is still in there," says the lady swapping.
"Ohh…we have some toys in there," Alex whispers.
"You have some what?" asked the STA agent with his loud voice.
"We have a dildo," she blushes.
"Oh, but it doesn't have a head. Hey, you knew there was a dildo in here that's why you gave it to me to scan you bitch," the lady yells at her friend who is quietly laughing.

Embarrassed is an understatement. It's not that we had a headless dildo in the suitcase but that this lady announced it to the entire airport. Can you imagine being judged by strangers for having a tiny headless purple dildo? It's way beyond embarrassing. The lady showed us mercy by not demanding that we pull it out to prove it's actually a headless dildo.

We were back in New York and this time making our way back to Asia but not without spending the night with one of my best friends, Michelle. Michelle and I have been friends since 2004, my first year at the University of the Western Cape. We were both leaders in the Impact Movement – The Christian campus ministry. She is the first person to tell me that our Christian friends were talking about my relationship with Rato. I told her the truth and she distanced herself from me. Not only did she distance herself, but she told other people as well. She said she needed "advice on how to deal with the situation". One of the people she told was best friends with Rato's boyfriend at the time and she told him. It was a mess. The gossip, the drama, the shame, the judgement – all just a huge mess. She moved to New York in 2008 where her entire worldview changed because of the power of travel.

"Khanyi, I'm so sorry my friend. I can't believe I behaved like that towards you just because you loved another woman. I want you to know that I don't think like that anymore."
"What changed?"
"My roommate here is a lesbian and is one of the best people I know."

This conversation right here made us closer than ever. It wasn't because she 'agreed' with me but that she was a big enough person to ask for forgiveness. Our friendship got so much better because of it. I had seen her a few times since then both in South Africa and in the U.S. It's become sort of customary for me to visit her whenever I am in New York and this time was no different.

When we came to New York this time, we stayed in her parents-in-law's apartment near Central Park. She had two deeply religious nieces visiting her from South Africa and had no space for us in her home. It's not that the nieces were religious that she didn't have space, she really didn't, she wasn't trying to hide her lesbian friends. She also had a two-year-old who wouldn't be able to sleep with all the noise Michelle and I make when we are together.

Robin, Michelle's husband, is one of those men who doesn't think taking care of his child is "baby sitting" but parenting. I once heard a man ask a friend of mine if her husband didn't mind babysitting their two daughters while she attends class. My friend replied, he is not babysitting, he is parenting. I've witnessed men being praised for spending time with their children as if that's something special for them to do. What a low bar to set for men. Robin was more than willing to stay at home and let us have his wife until the wee hours of the morning.

Robin's parents' wine collection is impressive. I literally put down the big suitcase, took my shoes off and bolted to the kitchen and started drinking. I invited my friend Shauna who I met at a hostel in the Philippines that year. Shauna was on a solo one-year world tour and I offered to let her couch surf in our house. I know what it's like to be a backpacker, every cent counts. She spent five days on my couch and was a pleasant guest. We kept in touch and I had to see her when we were in New York as she had taken a break from traveling. Shauna showed up with two bottles of wine and quickly caught up to our level of inebriation. Five wine bottles in and a countless number of weed blunts; Shauna starts:

"I've stopped wearing bras, they're so restrictive," she says drawing all eyes to her freed breasts.
"I would love to do that, but I think my boobs are too big," Michelle said.
"You can, just take it off, your boobs are beautiful," Shauna says unstrapping Michelle's bra.
"Well, I think we should all take off our bras then," Michelle insists looking for solidarity.

The next thing I remember is that we are all naked and I am part of what is to be my first orgy. Eight pairs of boobs, three mouths to kiss, me and Alex, Alex and Michelle, Michelle and Shauna. Michelle and I went for a little bit but when your friendship is at that level where you can't help feeling like you're sucking face with your sister, you stop. Shauna and I didn't go that long either because I was actually attracted to her and I knew those feelings were mutual. I was scared Alex would feel it and get jealous, so it was mostly me and Alex and me watching Alex with the other two.

I love watching two women together, but like when they are really together, not for show. Although I'm not opposed to a bit of lesbian porn. I just need to be in the right mindset when I watch it, otherwise the long nails can be a major distraction. If I am not drunk enough to not think about how painful it must be to have those nails up your vagina, then I will not enjoy the porn. It is also obvious that most lesbian porn is designed for male viewership. The girls are super girly with long perfectly done nails, high heels, and wear way too much makeup. A real lesbian should struggle to peel an orange and opening soda cans should be a mission. Anyway, what a wonderful way to end my time in backpacking in America; I finished with a bang, literally.

Chapter 17
Mabuhay

The first time we went to the Philippines was because of a vacation tossup. It was a choice between Indonesia and The Philippines. We had spent a month in Indonesia before and I had never been to the Philippines. Alex had been but only in the Luzon area. When she was there, she was advised to visit Palawan should she ever come back. She was told it was the most beautiful of all the islands and didn't have a lot of tourist, perfect place for a quiet vacation.

"Google it and see if we should go." I love how she said that as if it was up to me.

I googled and couldn't believe what I was looking at. It looked unreal, more like someone's imagined place but it was real, and I had to see it.

"Oh, that's where we're going. You can book the flights," we were on that Korean teaching salary.

I had read that most people speak English in the Philippines, but I didn't imagine that that would be basically everyone. Traveling in places where no one spoke English, I have become a pro at body language. I can fluently explain things without using any words. I knew all the gestures for asking for an ATM when we arrived at the airport in Manila, I confidently walked up to the security guard, ready to show off my practiced slow speaking while using my hands.

"Whherrree. iiisss..the..A.T.M?" I say gesturing what the machine looks like and what I want from it.

"Oh, just go straight when you get to the end, turn left. I don't think they'll work at this time, but you can try," he says smiling.

I was both embarrassed and excited. Embarrassed that I assumed that he wouldn't be one of the "most people" that speak English in the Philippines. How often do we do that though? Assume what people should and shouldn't know based on what they do for a living. We all prejudge, we all assign abilities to people solely based on the work they perform. For most of us it's a subconscious judgement but a judgment, nonetheless. I was excited to finally be in a country where people, and from that moment it was most people, spoke English.

I looked forward to making local friends and be part of the community because I could have conversations. After a full night sleeping on the airport floor, using our backpacks as pillows, we boarded our flight to Palawan island, landing at the island's capital, Puerto Princesa. The view of the island from the airplane is breathtaking. I knew that I was about to land in paradise. Getting to paradise isn't easy though, we had to get on a van for four hours to get to our first stop, Sabang where we spent the first week of our two-week vacation.

Sabang was beautiful, or rather it is beautiful, it's still there. It's a long stretch of white sand beach with resorts and reggae bars competing for tourists' attention. We stayed at the Forest Garden Resort, perfect for mid-range budget. Well, what do you call a budget that's slightly higher than backpacker but considerably lower than luxurious traveler budget? I think lower mid-range. This resort was beautiful, bamboo walls, a restaurant, the resort cat and a mouse here and there. The restaurant kept us there more than the cat, Tommy, who became our best friend. It was Milla's delicious food that made us stay the entire week.

Sabang is where I was first exposed to the disturbing phenomenon that is sex tourism. It had been something I knew theoretically but never seen. It was sickening to see the number of very old, white men holding hands with very young Filipino girls. I was more grossed out watching the interaction between the white men and their brown women. There is an obvious economic power dynamic that one notices through who pays and how the woman behaves. I watched one of the Filipina girls follow a man around the buffet table at one of the resorts.

We had decided to splurge a little bit and go to one of the luxurious resorts for dinner. This girl looked sad, she looked owned, like she wasn't allowed do as she pleases. She held her plate behind this overweight white man, put everything he was telling her to on her plate, she had no choice over what she wanted to eat. She belonged to him, and he displayed how much he was her owner. Young Filipino women, particularly poor young Filipino women, fall prey to these types of men. Our regular visits to the Philippines turned into a more permanent situation and I got to see a lot more of this at play. It is such a difficult situation to judge, some of the girls do it to provide for their families, others for a chance to go overseas to provide for their families. The need to provide for your family when you reach a certain age makes sense to me. I knew that it was expected of me as soon as I started working. It is not something I chose but something that I knew I was obligated to do. Thinking of it in those terms, I became less judgmental and more compassionate towards these girls.

We were deciding on staying in Sabang for both weeks of our vacation because we loved it so much, but our room became rat infested on what was supposed to be our final night. I am so scared of them, I don't want to see them, I don't care how big or small they are, they make me so squeamish. The Lord couldn't have come up with a better way of making sure we go to El Nido. Our uninvited creeps sent us packing that very morning. We took the evening van from Sabang to El Nido arriving there at midnight. The guest house we had booked was in a jungle and nothing exciting, the scary welcome from the aggressive dogs made it even worse.

We were certain we made a mistake leaving Sabang, but boy were we wrong. We woke up the next morning, ate the two slices of bread and three in one instant coffee provided by the guest house, and headed out to see where we were exactly. We made a few turns and there it was, El Nido. Limestone, upon limestone in the ocean, it was incredible. We wanted to be far from the main town but close enough to walk and that's why Makulay Lodge was the perfect spot. The room we booked was nothing impressive, a bed, cold water shower and a small desk. But the guy opened the door to the balcony where we had the view of Cadlao Lagoon and we were sold. Seeing that view made me understand that old church song, "how great thou art".

"O Lord, my God, when I'm in awesome wonder
Consider all the worlds Thy Hands have made
I see the stars, I hear the rolling thunder
Thy power throughout the universe displayed..."

The beauty of El Nido made me realize the majesty of the Universe. There was no other way to describe the sense of beauty and peace I felt looking at it. It was the first time I saw Alex crying over how beautiful a place is, she was so overwhelmed that tears just started rolling down her face. We had seen beautiful places but this, El Nido, it was magic.

Our accommodation was a few minutes' walk to a resort that promised an amazing breakfast and we wanted some of it. On the way to the resort, we walked past a local community and we were ready to make local friends. We had just registered our humanitarian organization, Agape Love Foundation that year and were dying for a project. We thought we would do something in Sabang but everything seemed good there in terms of schooling which is my passion. The second morning on our way to the best breakfast in town, Cadloa Resort, we saw small kids in school uniforms crossing the road to what we thought was an abandoned building.

"You don't think that's their school, right?" I asked.
"I hope not, that building looks abandoned, we should go talk to them today."

We quickly downed our perfect pancakes, crunchy bacon and sunny side up eggs and went to the school to find out what was happening.

"Hi, we just wanted to ask if this is a school." I enquired.

"Oh, yes, it is, we are a foundation phase learning center," says the smiling teacher.

We offered our help to make it more child friendly but in the most Western way of thinking about what a foundation learning center should look like. We promised play equipment, slides and swings, colorful things that the kids would love.

"That would be very nice, thank you, but right now, we need a wall and windows. The kids are scared to come to school when there's a typhoon and rain because the building is incomplete."

Oh man, we had fallen into the trap of humanitarian aid. Deciding for the communities what they should need instead of asking. I felt numb and a bit ashamed of how we handled that situation.

"Of course, how much will this cost?" asked Alex.

"I think about 10,000pesos (about $200)."

Okay, well we will come back tomorrow and see how we can help. On our way back to our room, we both agreed that we had the money on us, and we should help them. We wanted to surprise them that same day and just bring them the materials. That proved to be exceedingly difficult because it turns out that you can't just walk into any hardware store and buy sawali (woven bamboo) which is what the built half of the school was built with. We rode through town on our rented bicycles for the day going from one hardware to the next and we hesitantly went to the last hardware store.

"Hi, do you sell sawali," I asked.

"Why are you looking for sawali, are you building a house?" asks the older gentleman behind us.

"No, there is this school we want to help finish before we leave."

"Where is it?"

We explained the location of the school and his eyes went big.

"I am the project director for that school and community. Thank you so much for helping us. Please follow me, let's talk to them and tell them this good news."

We spent the rest of that afternoon sipping on buko juice (coconut water), answering personal questions and deciding when the work should start. Humanitarian work is basically helping other people, but the benefit is a selfish satisfaction. It feels so good to look at the joy people feel when you help them. The rest of our week was spent building walls and watching little people get excited about the cement on their school floor. It was such an act of love on our part and watching the community come together to work to make sure that they finish before we leave was amazing to watch.

Chapter 18

Blood, sweat and tears

We became regular visitors to El Nido before we finally decided to live there. The plan was to stay for six months while we regrouped after Costa Rica and decide what we were going to do next. We had online teaching jobs and the money we made was enough to sustain us. El Nido felt different this time though, there were so many people and the price of things had hiked up. It was a proper vacation spot now and it was busy. Trying to find a house was a nightmare, places were either too small, too expensive for what they were offering and for Alex, too far from the beach. A friend of ours pointed us to a Japanese woman who supposedly had a house she wanted to rent out. We found the Japanese woman and boy did I love her. Mishiko was a 70-year-old, small, Japanese woman running her big resort.

"Hey, you two are beautiful! Who are you, what do you want?" with a big smile.
"Hi, thank you, we are looking for a house to rent for a few months."
"I have a house, it's 20,000pesos a month, non-negotiable, do you want to see it?"
"Yes."
"Are you couple? It's two bedrooms but if you're couple, we'll make sure there's just one bed in the other room?"

Okay 70-year-old lady!

"Yeah we are."
"Okay, yeah I had a feeling. Okay, one bed it is then."

We followed her down a small road that led to a two-bedroom house built with four-inch plywood. The foundation was concrete and the rest of the house plywood and sawali. It was clean, new, had a functioning kitchen and was only a two-minute walk to the beach.
"We like it, but I'm worried about the noise with the plywood," I said.

158

"Sleep here tonight, and if you don't like it, you can move out tomorrow and you don't have to pay."

Sweet! We spent the night there and I was right. I am a light sleeper which means everything wakes me up – everything! The noise kept both of us up that night. It was the dogs that barked all night, the chickens who didn't know the proper time for being chickens, the drunk neighbors and the crying babies.

"We're not staying here babe," I complained.
"Okay, yeah it's very loud, let's look for another place."
We went to Mishiko, told her about our miserable night.
"Well, why don't you keep looking, if you don't find sleep here again but get earplugs, it's still free," why was she being so kind to us?

We kept the house hunting going for one more day with no luck, so we went to the pharmacy, bought earplugs, and properly moved in at Calaan with a kick ass landlady. I'm pretty sure this was the Universe conspiring on our behalf once again because Mishiko became our friend and having a friend who's lived in the town for fourteen years was a blessing. Three months into living in El Nido, we also got the itch to partake in its booming tourism. Our dream had always been to have an eco-resort and what could be better than building it in the most beautiful island in the world!

We, however, grossly underestimated the price of beach front lots and our hunt for land inside of El Nido became tiresome. We went on numerous boat trips to land we were promised was perfect and we got there, it was either not perfect or the family was fighting over it. We were just a young, hopeful couple, trying to start building an empire. People came to our house with pictures of their land or their friends' land or their cousin who lives in Manila's land. I was surprised by how many people knew we were looking. I think it was a matter of "oh, they've been here for a few months now, they must be looking for land".

159

We also knew we'd be staying longer than the planned six months because on our second month, we got our first pet together, Charlie. Our neighbor's dog gave birth and they offered us one of the puppies. I chose her. She was a day old, I picked her up and felt so much love. Charlie, finally! We'd talked about having a dog before kids and here she was. A small, black and white four-legged perfection, curling up in my hands, making me love her. Someone "mistakenly" took Charlie when she was about four weeks old. She was still too small for us to take away from her mother and so we'd go see her every morning.

One morning I showed up and she wasn't there. Oh, I raised hell. I went house to house, walked all over our neighborhood until someone said "oh, Jim took her to his farm". The day we had to wait for Jim to come back was too long. Jim knew that Charlie wasn't the dog he was offered, she had a collar.

"Sorry mam, I will go to the farm next weekend to pick her up," said Jim not knowing the crazy person he was talking to.
"I'm not waiting a whole week; you will go back today. I want to wake up to my dog in the morning." I said walking away.

Jim was knocking on our door with my Charlie at 8am the next morning. I then became known as the scary black lesbian lady in our small Taiyo village. Filipino men are intimidated by how tall and big I am, I'm sure Jim thought I was going to hit him if I didn't have my dog that morning. I am also well aware that the image of an angry black woman has made it all the way to Asia, and that's who my neighbors met that day and she scared the shit out of them.

During one of these "the perfect beach" trips, Alex was offered a boat. The land wasn't perfect, but the boat was. She came home all excited.

"Do you want a boat; we can buy it and turn it into a party boat. You've been talking about how you wanted a boat to drink and cruise with friends who visit, we can make it a business?"

"Yes, abso-fucken-lutely. Let's buy a boat!" I said jumping up for a kiss and a hug.

My twenty-three-year-old cousin had moved in with us at this point and this was a perfect thing for her. Pamela isn't good at showing emotions, you don't really know how she feels about anything. She giggles at the most awkward situations. The only time I saw her show a glimpse of sadness was when our young neighbor, Ilsa, told us what she wanted for her birthday.

"What do you want for your birthday, girl?" I asked.
"Nothing mam'Khanyisa, I just want to be happy. I just want one day where my family will be happy and not fighting," she said looking down.

Ilsa's family lived a bamboo fence away from us and we would hear everything. We would hear the drunk uncles staggering home every night, the loud drunken fights, and the morning throw up. Some days were just horrible, like when we were woken up by a crying infant at 4 a.m. and we went over; the parents weren't there. It was just the three girls, 11, 7 and 3 and the seven-month-old baby.

"Well, I can't give you that baby but we will bake a cake and have some fun," I said looking up at Pamela, she was struggling to hold back her tears and opted to go upstairs.

What they don't tell you about being an entrepreneur is that it is fucking hard. Maybe they do but no one told me, but I'm going to tell you; it is fucking hard. I was just a naive black lesbian woman, in a foreign town, with a lot of enthusiasm which by the way doesn't make running a business easy. We finally bought the boat that we thought was perfect for a party boat, we had help from Alex's dad and my aunt. On top of being overly enthusiastic, we were also too trusting and gullible – aren't all first time buyers though?

The guy who was the middleman for the boat sale charged us double the price...double! It's okay that he did, it's not okay that we didn't think to ask someone who has boats to look at it and see if we were getting what we were paying for. We were just so Bonga that El Nido is full of expatriates, and they were all willing to help us. One of them sent his mechanic and carpenter to the boat and they both said, "great boat but you're paying way too much". Our middleman, Kaka, had told us that the owners were in the states and there was no way we could get hold of them. After the boat's assessment our skins got just a little bit thicker.

"Kaka, we will not buy this boat until we talk to the owners, give them our phone number," I demanded.

A few hours later, my phone rang, and it was a Filipino phone number.

"Hi, this is Roy, Kaka said you want to talk to us, can you come to Seahorse dive shop?"

"I thought you were in the States?"

"What no, I've always been here, Kaka just wanted to handle the sale."

We found Roy who introduced us to his partner Mike, and they told us how much they wanted for the boat. Turns out that Kaka had plans to start his own dive shop with the other half. Everything was sorted out and we took the boat to our side of the bay. I can't explain the joy I felt having that baby parked there, all two-levels of her beauty. Our captain assured us that everything was fine and knowing nothing about boats, we believed him.

"Mam Alex is that your boat??!" our neighbor waking us up at 6 a.m. the next morning.

"Yes, what's wrong?"

"It's on top of corals mam, and it's not floating."

Holy fuck! I've had people talk about how they started their business with "blood, sweat and tears" and I'd always thought that is was a metaphor. It's not, it's literal, that boat had me bleeding, sweating and crying. The actual boat problems were nothing compared to dealing with the locals when we needed to register the business. We didn't know about the boat association that we had to be accepted into before getting our business permits. They were a new association that was introduced six months before we started our business and its rules were heavily enforced. This is what we faced every year, rules that changed overnight, administrators who didn't know the rules but wanted them followed.

The association is made up of other boat owners and you must get their approval before you could get your municipality business license. Foreigners were not allowed in the association, Filipinos who were not El Nido voters were not either. The Italian mafia has nothing on these guys. Okay, so you had to go to nine of these members, show them your complete boat papers and they each had to sign a piece on the sheet that says they allow you to join their gang. Only three signed and the rest refused because they thought our boat was too big and we were going to take all tourists. There is no amount of reasoning we could have done to convince them otherwise. We explained that we were more expensive than them and therefore were not their competition. We even sent one of our local friends to the toughest guy and he told her the truth about why he wasn't signing.

"He said he won't sign because he doesn't like the owner," she said looking away from me.
"I'm the owner he doesn't like, right?" I asked, unnecessarily.
"Yes, I'm sorry."

My aunt once told me that I was kind but I'm rough around the edges. She said it was a strange quality that I inherited from my grandfather. I know this about myself, I have been told this my whole life. I have been called sweet at times and other times I was told I had "fuck off" written across my forehead. The "fuck off" was usually pointed out by men who thought they were entitled to my smile. This man was different though. He talked to me once and decided that he didn't like me. I could tell this is what happened because I didn't like him either. He was a short little man with a face that said he drinks way too much alcohol and was on a power trip. Nothing I hate more than new money.

New money doesn't like to share, and new money is greedy. I internalized this man's hatred of me, I stewed in it for weeks and it drove me crazy. We were allowed to run the business for a few months while the paperwork was pending and the more we ran it, the angrier it made me. I was an angry person, all the time, a constant frown, sometimes I swear I could feel my forehead hurting. I went to bed angry, spent the day angry, went to bed angry and my relationship suffered. I became insufferable, a shell of woman, an angry black woman.

"One of the men in the boat association told me you intimidate him," said Mishiko one day.

Even though we had moved out of Mishiko's house at this point, she was still our friend and we went to her for everything. She was our superwoman. She knew everyone, had everything and was a wealth of information.

"Oh yeah, I didn't know I was intimidating." I joked.
"Well, you are and it's good. You are two women and it is good that one of you is intimidating, they know they won't walk all over you. You should keep it up," she was serious.

This advice didn't help with my rage. I was furious of feeling like I was treated like a black female business owner. All the French and Spanish business owners seemed to have it easy. Their paperwork was done, they seemed to just be floating through the town while we crawled. I began to be angry at the tourists who asked "how did you get this boat", "is it yours for real or you're working with someone", "oh I can't believe this is all yours" aahhhh make it stop. My rage was mostly because majority of our clientele is white, and I interpreted those questions as:

"How can you, black women, afford this boat?" and it drove me up the wall.

"You are always angry and it's starting to affect our relationship." Alex complained.

"How are you not angry, we have shitty boat captains, we're not being given our papers for silly reasons, I bet you it's cause we're black and gay." I yelled.

"How is being angry going to help us with this stuff?"

It wasn't helping and it was making me deeply dislike myself instead. I was becoming someone I didn't enjoy. There were days where I felt like giving up and selling the boat. I thought having a business would make me happy, but it was not but instead it was eating away at me. I felt rejected by the town, I could not believe that they were not more lenient to us after all the charitable work we had done for them. It was as if they owed me, they owed me kindness, they owed me fairness at the very least. Rather than getting any of that, we were being rejected; treated like outsiders which we were but where was that Filipino kindness? I struggled to reconcile the difference in.

"I'll work on it, I'm sorry."

We found our groove, I took up meditation and it helped with the anger, a lot. It helped let things bounce off me instead of soaking them in. I surrendered to the nature of the town and learned to grow a thick skin without being mean. Our business took off in ways that I did not even think were possible considering our rough start. We expanded from just running day tours to running three-day expeditions. We had people coming to El Nido for two days just so they can be on our party boat. Watching us grow, succeed, be happy was the greatest blessing. We usually joked around that we were God's favorites and this expansion was proof of that for me. We grew from boat business to building a glamping site on a beach, we called it Plumeria because of all the frangipani tree on the land. We were at the peak of our dreams, our baby (boat) was growing and from her, we were making more babies.

Chapter 19

Things fall apart

I was at the peak of my happiness and one day I woke up and felt that there was something huge coming. It felt like I was about to crash, that instead of a sliding hill on the side of the peak was just a sudden drop, a drop that I couldn't avoid. You know when you're swimming in the ocean, and all over sudden, it drops and you can't feel the sand under your feet anymore. This is what it felt like, like I had been swimming and that drop was coming. One of my favorite books is by the incomparable Chinao Achebe, "Thing Falls Apart." The story is of course gripping, I read that book in less than a week, but I must admit that it is not the story that sticks out for me, it is the title, Things. Fall. Apart. I got a tattoo on my arm this year, it's an incomplete infinity symbol and it's because I don't think anything is infinite, things end, things come to a point of being no more – Things Fall Apart. This morning, when I woke up feeling like a big wave was coming to crash on my shore, I thought about this, things really do fall apart, and nothing is infinite.

Things were different between Alex and I, emotionally. Everything felt different, the kissing, the snuggling even the hand holding. It felt like she was laboring to be with me, that she was with me because it's all she's been doing for the past seven years. I felt it because I was still so in love with her. We were fiancés at this point and the next conversation to be had was about getting married. We were starting to have all the things we'd dreamt of all these years; we had the dog, the business, the only thing we were yet to do was build a house and we had land for that. The next obvious step was to seriously discuss our wedding.

Charlie died. We came back from the States and she was coughing. Like any good dog owner who lives six hours away from the nearest vet, we consulted doctor internet and followed every instruction. After three weeks of trying everything and nothing helping, we finally decided it was time to take her to the vet. One of the perks of living in a third world country is that people will judge you for loving your dogs as much as you do but they will also let you ride on the public buses with them. The pharmacists in town were so used to us buying medicine for our dogs that they'd asked if we were buying medicine for them or ourselves.

We got on the bus with our sick Charlie, put her on both our laps petting her all the way to the vet. We'd come home to her foaming at the mouth one night and her eyes looking different. She'd always had sad eyes which made her really bad at begging. She wouldn't look cute; she'd just look sad. But this night, her eyes looked scared and violent. The wait for 5 a.m. was too long, that's when the first bus from El Nido to Puerto Princesa leaves. We arrived at the vet and he was sad to tell us that my Charlie had distemper and was going to die in a few days.

"She has to be very strong to beat this at this stage, it's too late now," said our vet looking at us as the tears started rolling.

We convinced ourselves that she was going to pull through, but I think we both knew she was not going to. I'd expect a phone call from Alex saying she'd died every time I left the house and every day, she made it was a miracle. She wasn't eating, drinking and the only time her tail would wag was when we put her on the grass to get some sun. My Charlie finally moved the night she died, Alex put her on her lap, and she ate a little bit, when she had had enough, she peed and died.

When I was repeating my last year of high school in Joburg, one of the girls came crying one morning because her dog had died. My mother died the year before and I was so angry at this girl for crying over a dog when people die. People, actual human beings die, and she was crying over some dog. She was one of the first thoughts that came to my mind when I was holding my Charlie, thanking her for the lesson in love. My Charlie would jump on the bed, lay on my chest for however long I needed her to and just be. She loved me when I wasn't performing, I didn't have to please her, she just loved me. Every time she saw me was a celebration for her, it doesn't matter if I was gone for a month or a minute, it was all the same.

"Where have you been mama, I've missed you," that's what I heard her say every single time I came home.

After Charlie died, we dug her grave in our shared yard behind the big mango tree right next to the river stream that flowed behind the premises. We dug the grave ourselves, at 10pm, with uncontrollable tears and we laid her to rest. She was gone. I never imagined myself loving an animal like I loved Charlie. I named her. She was my baby. Loss and grief are overwhelming, I learnt about loss and grief when my Charlie died. I learnt that we can't compare pain in the ways that we usually do – Charlie was not a human, but her death hurt as if she was. I still cry when I think about my Charlie, I'm crying now which makes writing this really hard. Things end, dogs die, nothing is infinite.

When we were in Korea, I cheated on Alex with a friend. I didn't have sex with her, we just kissed and made out a lot. I don't want to talk about what counts as cheating, but I think anything you aren't able to tell your partner is cheating. Anyway, we ended up having a very drunk three some with the friend, it wasn't good. Alex found texts and long skype call logs between the friend and I. She was about to leave me but decided not to and I stopped talking to the friend. It really doesn't matter that I stopped talking to her because the trust was gone and was to never return. We decided to have a "semi-open" relationship.

We could make out with other people but not have sex with them. This was easy to do when there was no one to make out with but it became a reality when we ran a party boat. We were surrounded by drunk, horny tourists. I was very insecure about men because well, they have a penis and Alex's bisexual and that's who she'd make out with. She was insecure about women because, well I'm gay and that's who I'd make out with.

"I think I want to sleep with men now, I still love you very much, but I'm physically attracted to them, and I think I want to try it. Let's fully open the relationship" she said one morning, pushing a knife through my heart.

"Okay, yeah, I think I can allow that." I felt myself go to a place of being very desperate.

Prior to this conversation, I had picked up on some flirting with her and the boat captain. The boat captain is married with two kids, attractive, and tall for a Filipino – a rare breed. We had had four terrible boat captains before him, and he was a God send. He treated the boat as if it was his and that's what everyone advised us to get, a captain that will think of your boat is his and this guy did. He hired his own crew, and they were amazing. It wasn't amazing to watch him and my fiancé flirt though. I watched her watch him sing at a Christmas party we'd thrown for our staff, and I was like, "Mhh that look was only meant for me." I told myself I was being crazy and pretended like it wasn't happening.

"What's happening with you and Andy?" I asked her one afternoon because she wouldn't shut up about him.

"Nothing, what do you mean?" she's such a fucking bad liar.

"Oh, there's something, what is it, you like him?"

"He's married…. and I'm not available," she looked away.

You know when your heart sinks and you can feel your left arm become numb, that's how I felt at that moment. I thought I was having a stroke.

"You can have your men sex, but the people who work for us are a no go," was my only condition when she brought up the subject.

"No, you are putting restrictions on an open relationship, it's not the point."

"No, I'm putting boundaries on an open relationship, it's what grownups do."

There's a line in this movie that we watched every year called Imagine Me and You, it's about a woman who leaves her husband for another woman.

"When something unstoppable comes, then there's nothing that can't be moved."

Every time I watched them interacting, I would think of that line. I was the thing that could be moved because something unstoppable was coming. I begged and begged, I reasoned, I threatened, I appealed but there was nothing that couldn't be moved.

"Okay then Alex, you've obviously decided that you don't want me anymore and you don't care but think about his wife and his children. This is not something you want to do to another woman" I said trying to appeal to her as a woman.

My words fell on deaf ears. I saw her look at me like I was talking to a brick wall, like nothing I said was going to change anything.

I knew we were done. When someone says, "I love you but I am not in love with you", you are done. The more I begged and asked her to shelve the breakup letters, the further I felt her drift. I was at a loss, and I didn't know what to do anymore. The captain was doing crazy boyfriend shit and I couldn't believe that my Alex was doing this to me. The truth is that being a good person doesn't exempt you from getting your heart broken. I live with the simple ideology of doing unto others as you would want done to you. I haven't always done that; I know there are people who think I'm a piece of shit out there, but I have tried my best. I have done my best to live with kindness and compassion; that is what I asked Alex for, kindness and compassion.

I called my friend Michelle, who by the way is my superhero.

"Michelle, my relationship is ending," I said in tears.

"Call my therapist, she'll skype you and I'll pay for your first session."

I started therapy and it was truly the best thing that anyone has ever done for me. Watching my relationship end and feeling like there was nothing I could do didn't hurt less because I was in therapy, it just didn't kill me. Did you know that your heart can be so broken that it causes physical pain just so you feel something else? It does, I started having toothaches, I keep a very rigorous dental routine and the most my teeth have hurt is when I chew ice. But this time, to create a diversion, my teeth would hurt. I'm still not sure about what could hurt more than hearing the love of your life say, "I love you but I'm not in love with you anymore." I was never going to not fight for this relationship. I had spent years building, breaking, rebuilding, loving and I wasn't going to give up. I fought until my therapist said, "what do you want?"

"I want my Alex back."
"Your Alex isn't coming back, what do you want?"
"I want this person to move out of my house, I don't like her."

Alex was at Plumeria, our eco-resort when I had this therapy session, so it was a good time for me to pack her things and tell her to find her own place. I knew that's what she wanted anyway. The resort was almost finished, and we were at a point where we could let our expedition guests camp there. We had an expedition that weekend and so she went to set it up and make sure it was somewhat guest ready. The plan was for me go to Puerto Princesa that weekend, but I didn't feel like being in the van. I was hungover from one of my close friend's 30th birthday parties and the thought of being on a van for six hours enduring the curves nauseated me. Instead of getting on the van, I started packing up her shit. She'd promised the Andy thing was over, but she was still not my Alex.

She'd been calling me all weekend, talking about how much she's loving being alone in Plumeria, how much she's missing me and the pride she felt for what we created. My heart felt unsettled that Sunday she was meant to come back and I just knew he was there with her. I topped up my motorbike with fuel and drove myself to what felt like my end.

I wanted to get there as fast as possible, but I also didn't want to get there at all. I accelerated my speed, and drove slowly, could not decide on the speed, didn't want to hurry to the end but also didn't want to prolong it. I kept thinking about everything Alex and I had been through in our seven years together, how she promised it was over and that she wouldn't do this to me. I kept saying that to myself on this traumatic drive, "She wouldn't do this to me, not after everything we've been through together." I debated between telling her I was coming or just showing up but settled on calling because I feared what I would find. It's as if I wanted to give her a chance to get her shit together. I stopped the bike, pulled out my phone and I was about to dial, it rang and it was her.

"Where are you?" she asked her voice shaking.
"I'm coming there, decided to pick you up," I said trying to be calm.
"Oh that's so sweet, we can spend the night if you want."
"Sure."

I started driving again feeling a bit more at ease. She didn't sound like she was doing something shady, she actually sounded like she was happy I was coming. My heart didn't stop pounding even with the light sense of ease. The closer I got to Teneguiban, the village where we boarded the boat to Plumeria, the weaker my knees got and sweatier my palms and, that numbness on the left arm came back. Not a pleasant state for motorbike driving. And there it was, the motorbike I bought him, well it was supposed to be a service motorbike for the businesses but he's the only one that drove it. It was there, in my parking space, it's as if this man was fucking everything that was mine. There was no escaping him, he was everywhere, my dreams, Alex's mind, my boat, and now my Plumeria. I parked next to it and pretended that I didn't know whose motorbike it was to the locals.

"Whose motorbike is that?" I asked Roxy who lives at the house where I park my motorbike and wait for a boat to go to Plumeria.
"Captain Andy, ma'am. He arrived this morning." Roxy replied unable to hide her discomfort.

It is a fifteen-minute boat ride from Teneguiban to Plumeria and when I got there, the tide was too low for the boats to go. As if I hadn't been through enough! I opted for the hour walk up and down a mountain. I walked, cried, felt my breathing stop, stopped walking, talked to myself, walked again, until I got there. I kept thinking about how different this situation would have been if I was a man. I imagined that it wouldn't have escalated to the point it did. A man would have kicked both their asses, fired Andy, didn't care if there was a boat captain or not. Or, this wouldn't have happened at all if I was a man.

Andy would not dare touch his sir's woman even if she seduced him. He would be too scared of the repercussions. But as biology would have it, I'm not a man, I allowed myself to be treated like shit. I didn't stand up for myself, I just asked for breakup conversations to be tabled, begged and got myself here, walking on a beach with the sun making me its bitch. My sweat and tears became best friends that day. I climbed over the last hill that blocked my view of Plumeria and was just in time to watch him be driven away on a boat. I felt their panic as they were organizing to get him out, the big scary lesbian was coming. I had all these things planned out in my head, was a lot of fucks but all I said when I got there was,

"That's it, I'm done, you can have it all, the boat and this, it's all yours, just book me a flight out of here. You brought me here just so you can break me and you did, you broke me, I'm done,"

Loving someone as much as I loved Alex is such a gamble, the pain is as intense as the love. It's the same way that my mother loved my stepfather. Like my stepfather, she knew I loved her like this. But, there was no way I was going to become my mother. I was not going to let loving her kill me. I was going to break, but I was not going to die.

She begged me to stay but I was done. I felt like such a fool, I felt weak, needy and utterly alone. We spent what would be our last night together and started walking back to the town as soon as the sun came up. She was a stranger to me; I didn't know this person. I had seven years of Alex, I was good at loving her, I was good at knowing her but this person walking next to me wasn't her. The long silences in between "I'm sorry" were painful, I didn't want her to hug me when I stopped to cry but she forced me. For the first time, in our relationship, her tears meant nothing to me. I didn't understand why she was crying; she was getting what she wanted. It is crazy that someone can make you feel so loved, so taken care of and yet break your spirit, make you feel unlovable.

There is no amount of "it's not you but me" a person can say that'll save your self-worth. The feeling of just not being enough, that you will always lack somehow. I was so hurt and so spaced out driving up that hill from Teneguiban back to El Nido, that God had to send some naughty kids to throw a rock at me to jolt me back to consciousness. I didn't see them but a big rock, out of nowhere landed on my right boob. It was a perfect landing, not on my face and not on the wheel because that would have caused an accident. It was a boob awakening, a quick "hey, this isn't worth your life," from the Universe.

I came back to the living and just planned how my day was going to flow. I was going to go home, hug Pamela and get the fuck out of this fuck town. That's what I called El Nido, a fuck town, other people called it Hell-Nido. That's what people do there, fuck. I'd say we do three things in this town "eat, work and fuck". During high season, it's a local to tourist fuck fest and low season is local to local fuck fest. I was not active in the fuck lifestyle. I was in a relationship!

Two weeks before that Plumeria incident, Alex shaved her lady bits, took her birth control pills in front of me. The fact that she shaved for this should let you know how inactive our sex life was. Also, any lesbian who finds hidden birth control pills in her house should know her girl friend is fucking a dude behind her back. I was trusting, or maybe trying to hold on because when she explained the pills, I let it go.

"Are these birth control pills?" I asked jokingly when I discovered tiny little pills hidden in a box of cough candies.

"Yes, you know we're open now, and I don't want to get pregnant," she says.

"You don't think this is something we need to talk about, why are you going on as if you're single?"

"It's my body, I didn't think it'd bother you."

"I think you knew it would or you wouldn't hide them?" I'm starting to yell.

"I'm sorry, I just wanted to be safe when it starts happening," she throws herself in my arms, the manipulative hug.

The day had finally come, and I was a spectator. Years of being told that I was more than enough sexually had come to this. "I'd never had an orgasm until I had sex with Khanyi" she'd drunkenly tell our friends. That used to make me feel so good, we had sex toys but our orgasms were not dependent on them. We hardly ever used them. We were now on our seventh year and the girl was desperate for some real-life dick. I have to say that I theoretically understand open relationships. I get that monogamy is a social construct and that by nature, we are non-monogamous.

However, in practice, I can't. I am not wired in that way; my jealousy doesn't allow me to be so open. However, I opened up with my Spinach (the nickname I had given Alex). She was Spinach because I love Spinach, I love it in all forms, steamed, grilled, blended in a smoothie. She was Spinach and I was Ducky, she called me that because she said I appear all calm on the outside, but she knows inside I'm freaking out, just like a duck. You know how ducks look calm and gracious, but you know they are paddling. I was a real duck this particular day. I had a composed on the exterior but wanted to scream.

"Why don't you love me anymore!!!?"

I thought loving her also meant allowing her to have those experiences that she craves. I also thought that she'd experience it and see how much men suck, how good she has it and that love can overcome any sexual desire. I was so wrong; she was so gone. I watched her get ready to have her man sex that morning and my heart felt like it was suspended from my chest that entire day. She didn't know who the man would be, but it'd be one of the camping tourists we had that day.

"This is still happening babe, I'll have my first man sex," she said.
"Okay."
I saw her the next morning and forced her to tell me in detail how it was.
"It was okay, a bit painful at first but luckily his penis wasn't too big," she laughed.
"Mhh, I'm not okay with this, I thought I would be." I confessed.
"Well, I'd rather breakup because it's not going to stop, we can be friends," she smiled.
"Let's breakup then."

I went home, packed a weekend bag, bought a bottle of wine, and drove to Sibaltan. It is a small town about an hour and a half outside of El Nido. I booked myself a room at this quiet bamboo structure lodge, threw myself on the bed and wept. I cried myself to sleep, woke up and wrote about how I was going to handle this breakup. One of the things on my list, after sex with many women, was that I will not drown myself in alcohol. I love to drink but I have never been someone who drinks to feel better.

I knew that alcohol doesn't make you feel any better, it just momentarily numbs the pain and I wasn't going to use it to numb mine. So, when I told my two best friends the day I was leaving, after catching the love of my life be shady with the boat captain, and they offered to get me sloshed, I said "no". I'm not going to roam the streets of El Nido defeated, broken; my grandmother didn't raise me like that. She doesn't get to break my heart and make me lose my dignity. We had pizza, I drank lemon juice and got on the evening van to Puerto Princesa.

Chapter 20
Where do broken hearts go? Thailand

My 4 a.m. uber drive from my hotel to the airport in Manila reminded me of a movie scene. I sat at the back and every song that came on the radio was significant to what I was going through. I cried the whole drive to the airport, wiped my tears to check-in and cried again waiting to board, wiped my tears to find my window seat and then cried myself to sleep, and woke up with more tears in Kuala Lumpur. I was making my way to Bangkok where I'd stay with my friend Van and lick my wounds.

Van and I met in Costa Rica where he was also a student at UPeace. He was one of the few openly gay men on campus and taught me a thing or two about resistance. Van led a walk out during a meeting with Ellen Johnson Sirleaf, President of Liberia. She gave a vague diplomatic answer about the country's stance on the LGBTQ community- homosexuality is still a punishable crime in Liberia. Unsatisfied with her reply, Van walked out inspiring a group of us to walk out with him. He is such a badass human with a big ass heart. Van was the first person I thought to contact that night in Plumeria. I needed to get away from my life in El Nido. I was unhappy and remembered that when I became an adult, I promised myself I would never stay where I'm not happy.

Although I was unhappy for a long while before I decided to leave, I regret staying as long as I did. I was so desperate to fix what was broken. I was embarrassed to breakup. After all we were Alex and Khanyi, my favorite couple. I was consumed by the notion of "what will people say?" and it held me hostage in a relationship that no longer served me, in a place that didn't want me. All of this, because I was overly concerned about the opinions of others. That Sunday in Plumeria was more than just a push to leave, it was a kick in the stomach. It was that kick that led me to text Van after years of not talking.

"Alex and I broke up, I need to get away, can I come to you," I asked.
"I'm sorry to hear that, when do you need to come?"

"I'll be there in two days."

"I'll see you then."

Van shares his beautiful two-bedroom apartment in Bangkok with his dog Ikkyu. I couldn't have asked for a better place to lay low at. I was with a gay and the gay had a dog! The universe's love for me is truly and utterly infinite. I don't have the words to explain the feeling of walking into that apartment and being greeted with one of Van's short hugs and Ikkyu's excitement.

"Welcome home, you don't have to tell me anything, just get some rest," Van said.

My swollen eyes must have communicated my pain and in the most genuine way of loving a friend, Van let me know that he was there in my silence but would be available when I find words. He let me take in all the love Ikkyu gave, and I received it all.

They say "to get over someone, you need to get under someone else" that's why after three days of hiding in Van's apartment, I got on Tindr. I was not ready for what I was getting myself into; the endless swiping, the bio reading, the matching and unmatching, it was a lot. I did however feel a little less alone, it was comforting to know that I wasn't the only one looking, the only one wanting and that feeling of being somehow connected kept me going until I made a match that I was willing to pursue.

I told my therapist that I was off black women, "they are my weakness, I want to date anyone but a black woman because I know I will want to be serious with one and I shouldn't be" I said. My therapist is good at telling you what to do but make it sound like she isn't. She "suggested" that I don't go on tinder and just take the time to heal from the traumatic experience I just had but like anyone with a broken heart, I wanted someone else to fix it. Forgetting everything I said about black women, the match I followed up on was with Aliya, a black American from DC, seems I have a thing for DC girls.

Alex and I never went on a "first date", we just started dating and so the whole concept was new to me. I sought help from my lesbian friends.

"Jossie, who pays for this date," it's a legitimate question, we are both women and queer, so we are not confined to heteronormative ways of dating.

"You do, Khanyi. You are the masculine presenting one and you should treat a lady," Jossie is a gentle lady, I should have known this is how she dates.

I decided that we would both pay for the date; she's a working woman and I will treat her as such. Aliya showed up to the date late, making me wait for fifteen minutes outside the hotel where the rooftop bar we were going to was. I hate waiting for people, I also hate making people wait for me. I think being late is disrespectful, but I wanted to go on a date and had to chill the fuck out. Aliya full figured, long dreads, beautiful, black woman. She is open, smiles a lot, and is loud. The first date went well, I thought, she was engaging but I didn't think she was gay, and I wasn't about to date another straight girl who "goes gay for Khanyi".

"Who do you date?" that's the best way I knew how to ask someone their sexuality.

"I date everyone but have mostly dated men up until now," oh she is looking to date and not just be friends.

I know you want to know who paid; I did. She came knowing that I would pay. She had exclusively dated men up until now and did not even know what "heteronormative" meant but I would soon teach her. Our second date was bad and that's only because she showed up almost an hour late, the restaurant she chose closed fifteen minutes after she got there, and I struggled to hide how pissed I was. She apologized, I forgave but I found out that the girl had some serious time problems, like the kind that could get one fired. Our third date was fantastic though.

We found the best rooftop bar in Bangkok, it's called Octave. Aliya organized weed brownies and we ate them while enjoying the best Thai mojitos in Thailand. After the happy, high and drunk, we went to Check-in 99 where we enjoyed live music and I finally had the courage to kiss miss Aliya. Thailand is known to be one of the countries that are open and accepting to the LGBT+ community. It is true, kissing in public as a lesbians was not frowned upon in Thailand, on the contrary, we got more stares from Westerners.

"Can I go to your house," go ahead now Khanyi, still got game!
"I've been living here for two years, and I've never had anyone come to my house," this wasn't a yes or a no.
"Well, I'm happy to be your first," damn smooth!

We got a taxi and made our way to her one-bedroom apartment. I didn't know that sex with a new person after having sex with one person for seven years, feels like sex for the first time. I was quite drunk and high so I'm assuming I did well but waking up next to a new person felt strange. Looking at someone else's sleepy face, smelling their morning breath was not as exciting as I'd imagined. I woke up not wanting to be there but how mean would leaving be? I stayed and turned down the morning joint Aliya was smoking.

"I had sex with a black woman." I told my therapist during our session.
"How do you feel about that?"
"I don't know, I don't remember the sex but the waking up, I didn't feel good." I confessed.
"Maybe you shouldn't be having sex with anyone, black or white,".

What was Nassimah suggesting I do, be alone with my sadness and my broken heart? Nassimah is the black, big eyed, queer goddess that is my therapist. The goddess I convinced myself overtime, I was crushing on. She saved my mind. Without Nassimah's advocacy for my heart and my mental wellbeing, I would have gone crazy. We started this journey of healing because of that traumatic breakup but we ended up unpacking everything about all my trauma. She helped me look at myself, really look at myself, my emotional addictions, my mommy issues, my childhood traumas, everything surfaced, and I had her in my corner helping me deal. I was so broken, and the thought of dealing with myself was terrifying so against Nassimah's wise counsel, I kept seeing Aliya.

Seeing Aliya didn't take away my pain, it wasn't healing but it was a much-needed distraction. I guess one could argue that she in fact, was my alcohol – numbing. She was the boost that my ego needed after months of feeling unwanted and unlovable. I was beginning to believe that it was me who was the problem, that however much I had to give, it was just not enough. Aliya didn't know this, but she was given a task she didn't ask for, putting back together the pieces of a broken heart. Trust a black woman to do just that, to pull you back together.

My favorite place to have sex was on her living room carpet, it was fluffy, small in length and width but big enough to fit two grown women. We would roll on that thing all night; body, sweat, weed, sex and it held it all. I will never forget the night we were having post-weed sex, high-sex, which is one of the best sex, and during climaxing in her arms, the sexy sex sounds turned to sobbing and Aliya, held me tighter and just whispered "I got you" and I truly felt 'got".

I was okay giving Aliya lesbian sex, which at first took her by surprise. She didn't know that another woman can make you orgasm like that or even that orgasms like that were possible. The number of orgasms that lesbians have during sex is insane. You think you're done, wait ten seconds and oops, there you go again.

Massive thank you to the universe for this magical gift that is the clitoris and once you find the person who knows how to take care of it, well then, you're good. Our sex was more than good, it was great, it was electrifying, but that's all I had to give Aliya, good, great, electrifying sex. She began to want more, a relationship, a label or some sort of promise and I had none of that to give. I had just had every promise made to me broken. One day, Aliya showed up with wine, cheese, whip cream, olives each with a heart on it. It all translated to her asking me to be her girlfriend, cheesy but so cute.

"I can be your girlfriend for the two months you have left in Thailand," she was moving back to the States.
"How about we revisit after two months and talk about a long-distance relationship?" Aliya said.
"I don't do long distance relationships."

The truth is that I couldn't do a relationship at all long or no distance, not with anyone. I was not even okay with the two months I was giving her, but I felt that was a nice thing to do. But the more I gave in those two months, the more she wanted. As the weeks drew closer to the end of her time in Thailand, Aliya wanted more of a commitment, she was "dating with a purpose". The pressure of having to make a bigger commitment began to weigh down on me. I was not ready for it and she knew that but still wanted what she wanted. Our time together ended when I went back to El Nido to properly leave.

I imagined a happy ending for us, but I ended up breaking her heart. Nassimah was right after all "hurt people, hurt people". Aliya came to visit me in El Nido, and I was different from the Khanyisa she met in Thailand. I was stressed, distant and very unavailable. There was no sex to be had, I wasn't feeling the same feelings for her I had felt in Thailand. I was wrapping up my life, a life I loved and that got ripped away from me. I was saying goodbye to Pamela, my businesses and my friends and she didn't fit. It was a difficult week for the both of us but mostly her. I wish I could go back in time and tell her not to come to El Nido.

Chapter 21

No endings here, only beginnings

In an attempt to get me to go back to El Nido, Alex came to Thailand to try to convince me to go back with her. This was before I went back, during my time with Aliya. We were sitting at the zoo in Chiang Mai when she confessed that she had actually been fucking the boat captain for months. The whole time I was made to believe that they were just attracted to each other, only kissed twice and when I caught them at the glamping sight, they'd "just kissed". I should have known right?! I didn't though, Alex had always told me the truth, always and it was difficult for me to suddenly think of her as a liar.

"I need to tell you something, maybe you can understand why this is happening" she said causing my heart to beat a hundred times faster
"You are having sex with him?"
"Yes, but I'm going to stop," she starts crying.
"I want you to leave, pack your bags, find your own hostel and go back to El Nido," I said after minutes of silence.

I was once asked if I know how to be angry and the answer is that I think I don't. How else would I explain being on the same plane with Alex, sitting next to her on our flight back to Bangkok? How I let her hug me after everything she put me through? How I still talk to her to this day? I just don't know if I know how to be angry. I feel anger but I just don't think I know how to express it.

We flew back to Bangkok that Monday morning knowing that our friend Minaj would be waiting for us. When we met him, Minaj had spent eight months in Koh Phangan learning to be a sacred healer. I was so happy to see him even though he had lost so much weight. He'd just come out of a ten day fast and was skin and bones. Minaj's, now Muira, gift is picking up on people's energy and helping them release emotional trauma. He quickly picked up on the energy between Alex and I and started working.

184

"I can't be in the same room with you two, one of you has to go," Muira said after giving Alex a session.

"Well, I live here, so I guess she needs to go."

"She will go to Koh Phangan to meet my teacher."

Two more sleeps and Alex was on a bus to Koh Phangan. I had a session with Muira and it was by far the most intense, spiritual thing I've ever done and I used to speak in tongues when I was a Christian but this was even more intense. I laid on my bed and he had me repeat a few sentences. Each sentence dealt with an issue that I was dealing with from being abandoned by God to how angry I was at my mother. I resisted, I cried, and I felt such a beautiful sense of peace when it was all done. Muira then instructed that I should be alone for a few hours, I should not drink or have sex for three days. He said I was "open" and needed time to process what I'd experience. I drank wine that same night and got on an uber to have sex with Aliya. I didn't mean to disrespect my friend's work, but I was not okay with being so...alone.

"Raaman, Muira's teacher, wants you to come here tomorrow." Alex via text.

"Tell him I'll come after you leave."

"He says he'd like to see us together, wants to know what happened to you when you were seven."

"I'll be on the bus tomorrow."

I went through a traumatic experience at seven years old. I was sexually molested by an uncle, and I remember everything about that day. I was playing with my cousins outside and Eric, the uncle, called me to his room, put me in his bed and sexually assaulted me. I remember the breathing, the humping, I remember how he froze and then told me to not tell anyone.

"Ungaxeleli mntu ngalento uzobethwa nguKuku" (Don't tell anyone about this, Kuku will hit you)

He played on the fear I had for my grandmother very well. She wasn't a sweet old woman, she used to hit me for almost everything. She was so quick to anger and never available to listen. Her rearing style was putting the fear of God in you, well the fear of her. My silence after the sexual assaults, there were many, was that I was afraid of her. I was afraid that she would say I did something wrong; I knew she would find a way to make me feel responsible for it.

Alex knew about the sexual assault, but she doesn't know the age. I was intrigued by the fact that this guy knew, and I had to see him. The journey from Bangkok to Koh Phangan by bus is very long, eight hours on the bus and four hours on the ferry. Way too long for my level of anxiety and impatience. Alex booked us a room in a very nice resort, she knows how much I love nice things and in trying to impress me, she spent some cash on a resort. Her goal was to get me to be her best friend. How fucked up is that? The resort is only a two-minute walk to the beach, has a swimming pool and the food is so good. I loved Koh Phangan, the town is small, beautiful and screams hippie. It's the dreaded white people, the vegan restaurants, the elephant pants and the number of yoga studios that makes it a hippie town. The tension between the two of us settled as soon as we said hello taking away my fondness of this new town.

"What am I doing here?" I asked.
"We'll go to the sacred house tomorrow and you'll see."
The S.A.C.R.E.D. house is where the guru and his devout followers do their sessions. The Sunday was a group session and it was more like a love orgy. The guru looks exactly how I'd imagine a guru to look like. He's a tall, thin, long grey hair, slow spoken man. There was a bonfire when we arrived, a skinny slow walking woman walked over, and I watch her and Alex share a very long hug. She then turned to me, introduced herself and gave me the same long, tender hug. I watched all of them greet each other like that, long hugs that end with a content sigh.

"You can take a fire bath if you'd like," no explanation.

I followed Alex around as she did this woo-woo practice, we turned side to side, letting our bodies feel the heat. The peace and solitude of this place is hard to explain. I immediately felt the need to speak softer, move slower, breathe deeper and be fully present, fully here. We were all ushered inside to begin the session. It was very similar to the session I had with Muira, only this time it was fourteen of us and there was music in the background. All the songs were about love, beautiful, spiritual love songs I'd never heard before. We all repeated everything Raaman was saying, some meant nothing to me, but others made me cry. I cried a lot. After the meeting, Alex came for a hug and my heart was at such peace that I returned it. It was two days of being with her without the pain I was feeling.

My next session was with Kumari, the skinny brunette who gave long, tender hugs. I knew the drill now, lay down, repeat the sentences and release. It was different with her, she laid out some pictures and said they were her spirit guides. She asked me to invite my spirit guides to the session for guidance. I called out to my grandfather and my cousin Asanda. Asanda died from HIV/AIDS when she was 24. Her and I had a love-hate relationship. The only time I felt that she was my cousin is when she would fight the bullies for me. She was tall and big and was known in the town as "Queen Latifah". She would fight the bullies but then when we got home, she would bully me.

I was always her quiet, uncool, shy poor cousin. When we were teenagers, she was the rebellious child; her mother used to go pick her up from her boyfriend's place. It was always drama when Asanda had a boyfriend. She didn't make a secret of it, she did whatever the fuck she wanted and dealt with the consequences later. I, on the other hand, was the angel, the "do as she is told" girl. You can't take away the joy I had when I overheard her mother scream at her "why can't you be more like Khanyisa?" I was the exemplary family member, I became the child everyone wanted their children to be like; obedient, church going and born again. What they didn't know was how much pain I had under all of that "goodness", how much I was hurting and hiding.

Asanda called my aunt when she was extremely sick living with her boyfriend in Port Elizabeth. She told her she had HIV and she wanted to come home, but her doctor asked her to wait for the ARVs (Antiretroviral drugs). I was on winter vacation and spending the month between Cala and Queenstown. I made sure I was in Cala when she came home because I wanted to see her, take care of her. My eyes couldn't believe what they were looking at; my big boned, tall, full of life and spark Asanda had rapidly deteriorated. My grandmother boiled some aloe for her to drink; she calls it "uzifo zonke" which loosely translates to (all diseases). My grandmother swears by aloe vera, there is no ailment you can have that it won't heal. I got Asanda ready for a trip to hospital the next morning where she died two days after.

It shocked me that I didn't call out to my mother but made sense during the session. I was angry at her, every time I was asked to release something, she'd done I would close my fists as if I was about to fight her. I didn't want her to be my spirit guide. The session addressed that rage and left me with peace about my relationship with her. I released the romanticized idea of what a mother should be and looked at her as a human who was doing what she could to survive. I understand now that I wasn't only asking my mother to choose between me and her husband but me, her husband and her three children. She had to find ways to accommodate all of us, I opened my eyes to the fact that she had a family that she needed to think about as well. Her husband made more money than her, so she couldn't just up and leave. This healing session was vital in finding some closure with my mother and I am grateful.

"Someone is touching my feet," I said to Kumari with my eyes closed and wondering who the third person was.
"Okay, what does that touch remind you of?"
"My grandfather, he used to play with my feet," I said sobbing.
"Your grandfather is here; he wants you to know that he never left you and you are okay."

This was the first visitation I've ever had from my grandfather and timing couldn't have been more perfect. I was heartbroken, I needed him. My grandfather was my fiercest protector and I needed him to protect my heart. I was so happy that he showed up, let me know that I was okay, and I can talk to him whenever I want. When I left the Christian religion, I opened myself up to having other spiritual experiences that were not boxed in any religion. This is exactly what this was, a refreshing of my spirit without the dogma of religion. Like so many people who live outside the boundaries of their socialization, I cannot and will not reconcile with the Christian God, but I do know that there is something/someone way bigger than me. I call God a woman actually and I know She is with me all the time.

After Koh Phangan, I've been living like the only thing I know for sure is that SHE loves me fiercely. I understand that my spiritual walk doesn't have to be labelled as anything and doesn't have to be boxed in any religion. I celebrate that my walk with Her is not defined by guilt and shame. I never thought that that level of spiritual liberation could be possible.

My journey has led me into incredible places and amazing human experiences. I now find myself teaching English at a monk University in the outskirts of Bangkok, Thailand. The pain of ending what I thought was forever brought me here, but I am not bullshitting when I say that I thank the Universe for the pain, I am grateful that this traveling experience has brought me to the small town of Salaya, teaching monks. I am learning that we are all just people, having a human experience. I learn this even from the monks. I was excited when I heard that my students were 40 percent monks because I thought they would be well behaved.

I had to change that thought so fast my head spun. Some of them are so naughty, they giggle at sexual jokes (they're celibate), they are loud, they love playing games and competing. I "caught" one of my monk students watching a video of girls at a club on his phone. He was breaking every monk rule I knew. They are supposed to be celibate, not listen to music and definitely not watch girls in short little skirts dancing at a club. I say "caught" because he started apologizing profusely as if I was going to report him to someone. His reaction took me way back to my years of being a born-again Christian, where I broke all the rules and the guilt that brought me. I was again reminded that no matter how much we insist on our differences, that even the things we think should divide us are in so many ways, similar.

I feel like the Universe has pulled me here just to say, "see, you are just a person, having a person experience just like these monks." I am also learning that I will never again play second place to anyone when it comes to this life experience. One of the things that terrified me about ending my life with Alex was the daunting question of "what now?". My life had orbited around hers for so many years and the fear of navigating through life, as just me, was beyond scary. It is so easy to lose ourselves in the comfort of a relationship.

We forget our aspirations, what makes us tick, what we love, what turns us on because we are too busy trying to keep someone else's light ablaze. We do this at the cost of diming our own light. May we all form an alliance of radical self-love – loving ourselves in a way that is always self-choosing. I truly know that the pain of losing her led me back to myself, back to who I was introduced to in South Korea, and she is a fucken badass. I also know that this journey is one that fluctuates, where there will be times when I forget again, and the Universe will once again have to remind me of who I am. I only hope that when it happens again, the lesson will be less painful and perhaps even pleasurable.

I must confess that it is difficult to finish this book because I am not done. I plan on traveling this beautiful world of ours until my very last breath. I intend on living as a Traveling Black Lesbian. May you be blessed with the invaluable opportunity to see this world of ours as well. When you do, may you be reminded that you were never lost, you were always right there, waiting to return back to *you*.

Love yourself and be kind.

ACKNOWLEGEMENT

To the teenager who birthed me, the poor priest and prison cook who raised me and the perceived heroes and villains of my story, thank you. Each of you taught me something valuable, something beautiful and something extraordinary. My life is a lesson on love, kindness, and courage.

www.ingramcontent.com/pod-product-compliance
Lightning Source LLC
LaVergne TN
LVHW051553080426
835510LV00020B/2968